Atlas _{of} _{the} Maldives

ޢަލިފުޅު

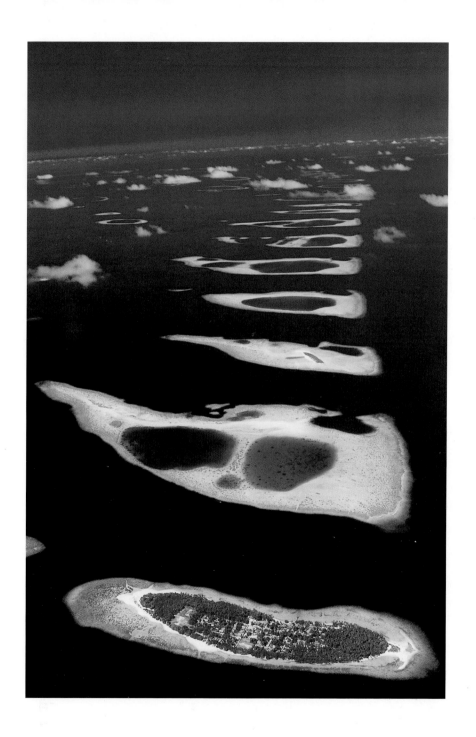

Atlas of the Maldives, 2007
ISBN 978-1-876410-43-8
Publisher: Atoll Editions, PO Box 113,
Apollo Bay, Victoria, 3233, Australia
www.atolleditions.com.au
email: info@atolleditions.com.au
Research by Tim Godfrey
Finished Art by Munch Design
First Published as Malways,
Maldives Island Directory in 1996.
Second Edition 1998.
Third Edition 1999.
Fourth Edition, Atlas of the Maldives 2004.
Copyright © Atoll Editions

The 5th Edition of Atlas of the Maldives includes a number of island changes caused by the December 26th, 2004 Tsunami. Details of these changes are listed on page 13. Proposed resort islands and islands under construction have also been updated. There have been some changes to the atoll maps, such as the increased number of communications towers and Atoll Editions is grateful to individuals, businesses and government organizations that have provided details of these changes. These changes are occurring all the time and we invite readers to notify us of any observations they feel should be included or changed in future editions of the Atlas.

We would like to acknowledge permission granted by the UK Hydrographic Office for the use of their Uligamu island chart. We are particularly grateful for the support of the Ministry of Transport & Civil Aviation, Ministry of Atolls Development, Ministry of Construction & Public Works, Ministry of Tourism, Ministry of Fisheries, Agriculture & Marine Resources, National Centre for Linguistic & Historical Research and the Hulhumalé Development Section. Also, to our sponsors Dhiraagu, Island Aviation Services and Maldivian Air Taxi.

Photo acknowledgements

Front cover: photos top left & right - **Tim Godfrey**
photos top middle & main - **Sigurd Schjoett**
Back cover: **Adrian Neville**
Title page: **Sigurd Schjoett**
Page 8: **John Callahan**
Page 9: **Sigurd Schjoett**
Page 12: **Adrian Neville**
Page 13: **Shaahina Ali**
Page 15: **Space Imaging**
Page 16: photo 1 - **National Centre for Linguistic and Historical research**,
photos 2, 3, 4, 5 & 6 - **Tim Godfrey**
Page 17: photos 1, 4 & 6 - **Sigurd Schjoett**
photos 2 & 5 - **Yassim Hameed c/o Island Aviation Services**
photo 3 - **Space Imaging**
photo 7 - **Tim Godfrey**
Page 18: photos 1, 3, 4 & 5 - **Udo Kefrig**
photo 2 - **Tim Godfrey**
Page 19: photo 6 - **Kimmo Hagman**
photo 7 - **Simon Rogerson**
photos 8 & 10 - **Udo Kefrig**
photo 9 - **Musthag Hussain**
photo 11 - **Tim Godfrey**
photo 12 - **Antonio Frisca**
photo 13 - **Brigitte Schmpera**
Page 20: photos 1, 2 & 6 - **Sigurd Schjoett**
photos 3, 4, 5 & 7 - **Tim Godfrey**
Page 21: photo 1 - **John Callahan**
photos 2, 3 & 5 - **Sigurd Schjoett**
photo 4 - **Yassim Hameed c/o Island Aviation Services**
photo 6 - **Tim Godfrey**
Page 22: photos 1-6 - **Tim Godfrey**
Page 23: photos 7-12 - **Tim Godfrey**
photo inset top right - **Space Imaging**
Page 25: **Space Imaging**

EXPLANATION OF SYMBOLS FOR ATOLL MAPS

DEPTH CONTOURS

Reef				Airport, international
0m - 20m				Airport, regional
20m - 50m				Port & starboard lights
50m - 1000m				12 Mile light
1000m - 2000m				2 Mile light
Deeper than 2000m				MIFCO (Fishing boat lights)
				Fishing boat route
THULUSDHOO	ATOLL CAPITAL			Fishing island
Dhiffushi (501)	Population over 500			Picnic island
Olhuvelifushi (499)	Population under 500			Agricultural island
Holiday Island	Resort island			Marina
Vammaafushi	Uninhabited island			Anchorage
				Rock, awash
MIYARU KANDU	Protected Marine Areas			"Archaeological site"
	Atoll administrative boundary			Regional hospital
				Atoll hospital
Oceana, July 19, 1917	Wreck			Mosque
(45m) (45m)	Communications towers			Tsunami safe islands
	Island Aviation Services			Islands to be relocated
				Islands most affected by tsunami

Atlas of the Maldives

Contents

"Dictionary"

air taxi / ear taeksi / noun (C) short form for Maldivian Air Taxi, an airline in the Maldives operating Twin Otter seaplanes, in the business of transferring tourists to and from their resort destinations; *Air Taxi maintains an uncompromising level of safety · The staff at Air Taxi are friendly and professional · In operation since 1993, Air Taxi is reliable, dependable operator in the Maldives.*

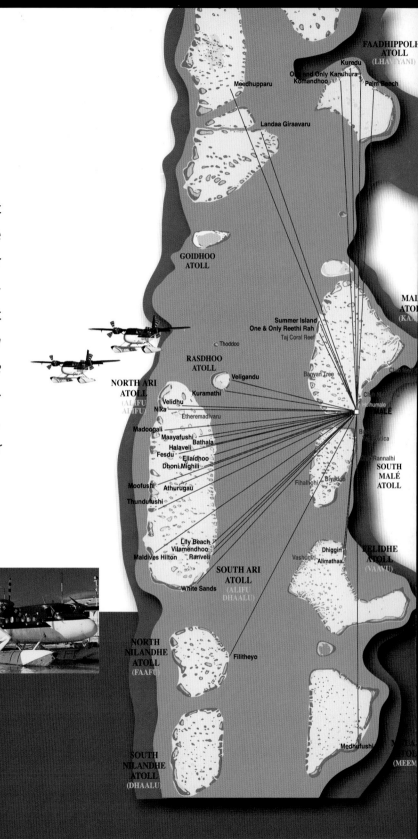

MALDIVIAN AIR TAXI

Maldivian Air Taxi (Pte.) Ltd. – P.O. Box 2023 Male' Republic of Maldives – Phone: (+960) 31 52 01 – Fax: (+960) 31 52 03 – mail:mat@mat.com.m – www.mataxi.com

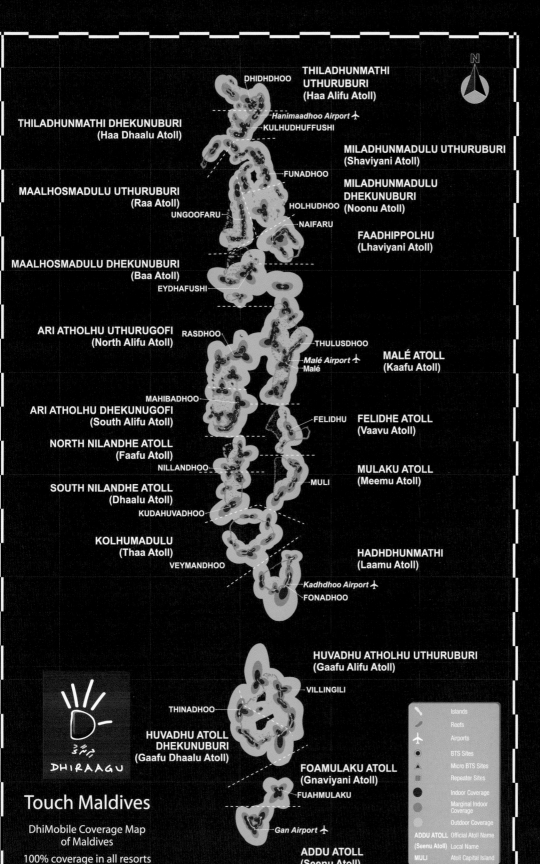

THILADHUNMATHI
UTHURUBURI
(Haa Alifu Atoll)

DHIDHDHOO

Hanimaadhoo Airport ✈
KULHUDHUFFUSHI

THILADHUNMATHI DHEKUNUBURI
(Haa Dhaalu Atoll)

MILADHUNMADULU UTHURUBURI
(Shaviyani Atoll)

FUNADHOO

MILADHUNMADULU
DHEKUNUBURI
(Noonu Atoll)

MAALHOSMADULU UTHURUBURI
(Raa Atoll)

HOLHUDHOO

UNGOOFARU

NAIFARU

FAADHIPPOLHU
(Lhaviyani Atoll)

MAALHOSMADULU DHEKUNUBURI
(Baa Atoll)

EYDHAFUSHI

ARI ATHOLHU UTHURUGOFI
(North Alifu Atoll)

RASDHOO

THULUSDHOO

MALÉ ATOLL
(Kaafu Atoll)

Malé Airport ✈
Malé

MAHIBADHOO

ARI ATHOLHU DHEKUNUGOFI
(South Alifu Atoll)

FELIDHU

FELIDHE ATOLL
(Vaavu Atoll)

NORTH NILANDHE ATOLL
(Faafu Atoll)

NILLANDHOO

MULAKU ATOLL
(Meemu Atoll)

MULI

SOUTH NILANDHE ATOLL
(Dhaalu Atoll)

KUDAHUVADHOO

KOLHUMADULU
(Thaa Atoll)

VEYMANDHOO

HADHDHUNMATHI
(Laamu Atoll)

Kadhdhoo Airport ✈
FONADHOO

HUVADHU ATHOLHU UTHURUBURI
(Gaafu Alifu Atoll)

VILLINGILI

THINADHOO

HUVADHU ATOLL
DHEKUNUBURI
(Gaafu Dhaalu Atoll)

Touch Maldives

DhiMobile Coverage Map
of Maldives

100% coverage in all resorts

FOAMULAKU ATOLL
(Gnaviyani Atoll)

FUAHMULAKU

Gan Airport ✈

ADDU ATOLL
(Seenu Atoll)

DHIRAAGU

	Islands
	Reefs
✈	Airports
⊙	BTS Sites
▲	Micro BTS Sites
■	Repeater Sites
	Indoor Coverage
	Marginal Indoor Coverage
	Outdoor Coverage
ADDU ATOLL	Official Atoll Name
(Seenu Atoll)	Local Name
MULI	Atoll Capital Island

Last updated on 1st November 2006

5

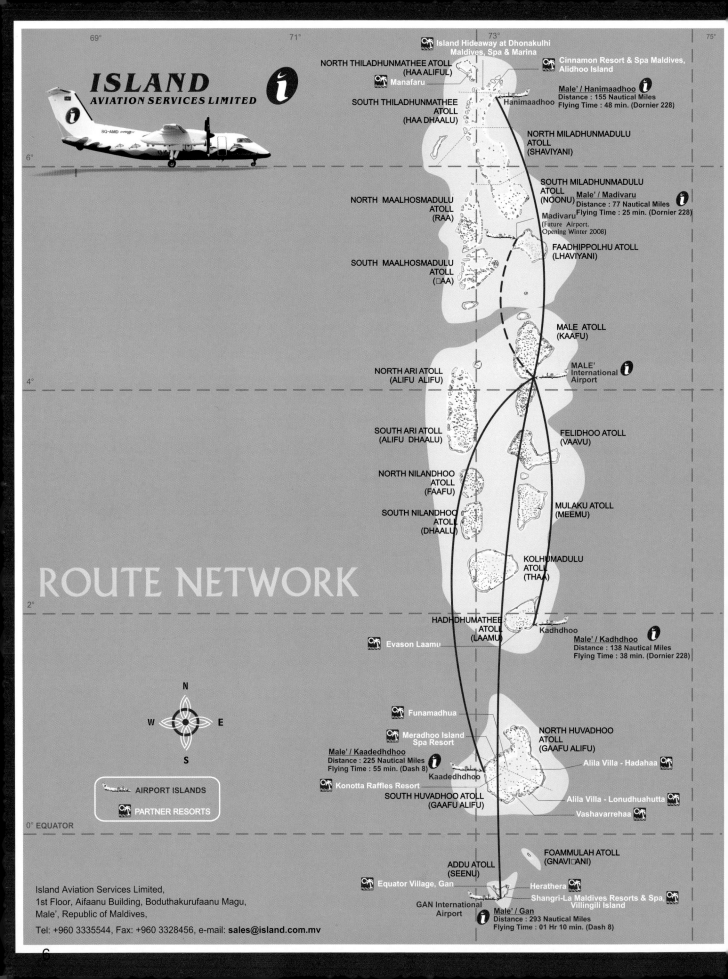

ISLAND
AVIATION SERVICES LIMITED

ROUTE NETWORK

Island Hideaway at Dhonakulhi
Maldives, Spa & Marina

NORTH THILADHUNMATHEE ATOLL
(HAA ALIFU)

Cinnamon Resort & Spa Maldives,
Alidhoo Island

Manafaru

SOUTH THILADHUNMATHEE ATOLL
(HAA DHAALU)

Hanimaadhoo

Male' / Hanimaadhoo
Distance : 155 Nautical Miles
Flying Time : 48 min. (Dornier 228)

NORTH MILADHUNMADULU ATOLL (SHAVIYANI)

SOUTH MILADHUNMADULU ATOLL (NOONU)

Male' / Madivaru
Distance : 77 Nautical Miles
Flying Time : 25 min. (Dornier 228)

Madivaru
(Future Airport.
Opening Winter 2008)

NORTH MAALHOSMADULU ATOLL (RAA)

FAADHIPPOLHU ATOLL (LHAVIYANI)

SOUTH MAALHOSMADULU ATOLL (□AA)

MALE ATOLL (KAAFU)

NORTH ARI ATOLL (ALIFU ALIFU)

MALE' International Airport

SOUTH ARI ATOLL (ALIFU DHAALU)

FELIDHOO ATOLL (VAAVU)

NORTH NILANDHOO ATOLL (FAAFU)

SOUTH NILANDHOO ATOLL (DHAALU)

MULAKU ATOLL (MEEMU)

KOLHUMADULU ATOLL (THAA)

HADHDHUMATHEE ATOLL (LAAMU)

Kadhdhoo

Evason Laamu

Male' / Kadhdhoo
Distance : 138 Nautical Miles
Flying Time : 38 min. (Dornier 228)

N
W E
S

Funamadhua

Meradhoo Island Spa Resort

Male' / Kaadedhdhoo
Distance : 225 Nautical Miles
Flying Time : 55 min. (Dash 8)

NORTH HUVADHOO ATOLL (GAAFU ALIFU)

Alila Villa - Hadahaa

Kaadedhdhoo

Konotta Raffles Resort

SOUTH HUVADHOO ATOLL (GAAFU ALIFU)

Alila Villa - Lonudhuahutta

Vashavarrehaa

AIRPORT ISLANDS

PARTNER RESORTS

0° EQUATOR

FOAMMULAH ATOLL (GNAVI□ANI)

ADDU ATOLL (SEENU)

Equator Village, Gan

Herathera

Shangri-La Maldives Resorts & Spa,
Villingili Island

GAN International Airport

Male' / Gan
Distance : 293 Nautical Miles
Flying Time : 01 Hr 10 min. (Dash 8)

Island Aviation Services Limited,
1st Floor, Aifaanu Building, Boduthakurufaanu Magu,
Male', Republic of Maldives,

Tel: +960 3335544, Fax: +960 3328456, e-mail: **sales@island.com.mv**

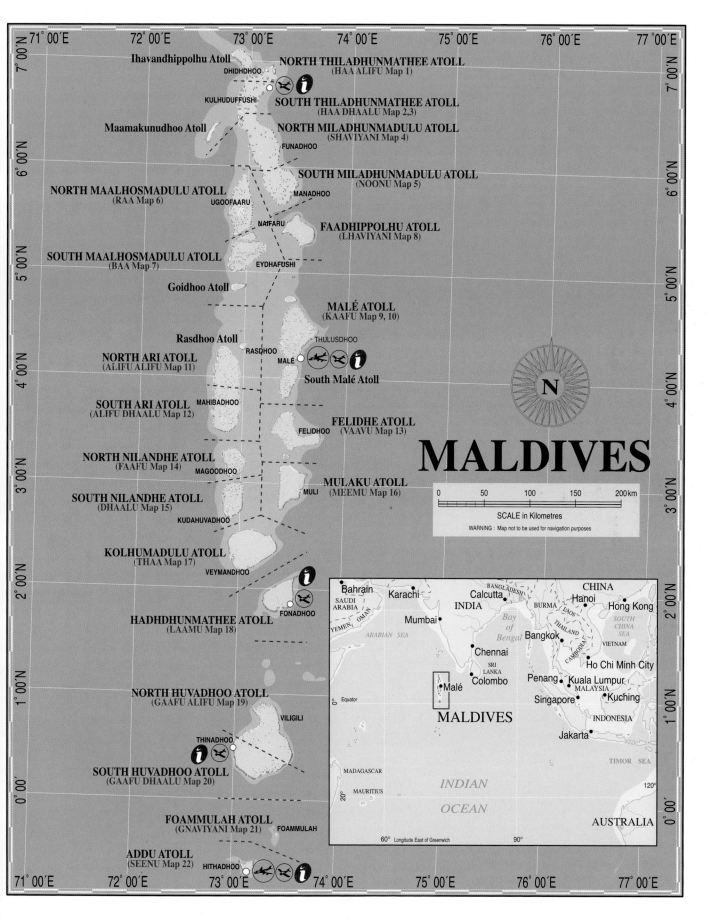

MALDIVES

Ihavandhippolhu Atoll
DHIDHDHOO

NORTH THILADHUNMATHEE ATOLL
(HAA ALIFU Map 1)

KULHUDUFFUSHI

SOUTH THILADHUNMATHEE ATOLL
(HAA DHAALU Map 2,3)

Maamakunudhoo Atoll

NORTH MILADHUNMADULU ATOLL
(SHAVIYANI Map 4)

FUNADHOO

SOUTH MILADHUNMADULU ATOLL
(NOONU Map 5)

NORTH MAALHOSMADULU ATOLL
(RAA Map 6)

MANADHOO

UGOOFAARU

NA1FARU

FAADHIPPOLHU ATOLL
(LHAVIYANI Map 8)

SOUTH MAALHOSMADULU ATOLL
(BAA Map 7)

EYDHAFUSHI

Goidhoo Atoll

MALÉ ATOLL
(KAAFU Map 9, 10)

Rasdhoo Atoll

THULUSDHOO

RASDHOO

NORTH ARI ATOLL
(ALIFU ALIFU Map 11)

MALÉ

South Malé Atoll

SOUTH ARI ATOLL
(ALIFU DHAALU Map 12)

MAHIBADHOO

FELIDHE ATOLL
(VAAVU Map 13)

FELIDHOO

NORTH NILANDHE ATOLL
(FAAFU Map 14)

MAGOODHOO

MULAKU ATOLL
(MEEMU Map 16)

MULI

SOUTH NILANDHE ATOLL
(DHAALU Map 15)

KUDAHUVADHOO

KOLHUMADULU ATOLL
(THAA Map 17)

VEYMANDHOO

HADHDHUNMATHEE ATOLL
(LAAMU Map 18)

FONADHOO

NORTH HUVADHOO ATOLL
(GAAFU ALIFU Map 19)

VILIGILI

THINADHOO

SOUTH HUVADHOO ATOLL
(GAAFU DHAALU Map 20)

FOAMMULAH ATOLL
(GNAVIYANI Map 21)

FOAMMULAH

ADDU ATOLL
(SEENU Map 22)

HITHADHOO

| 0 | 50 | 100 | 150 | 200 km |

SCALE in Kilometres

WARNING : Map not to be used for navigation purposes

N

Bahrain
Karachi
SAUDI ARABIA
YEMEN OMAN
ARABIAN SEA
Mumbai
INDIA
Chennai
SRI LANKA
Colombo
Malé
MALDIVES
Equator

Calcutta
BANGLADESH
BURMA
LAOS
Bay of Bengal
Bangkok
THAILAND
CAMBODIA
VIETNAM

CHINA
Hanoi
Hong Kong
SOUTH CHINA SEA
Ho Chi Minh City
Penang
Kuala Lumpur
MALAYSIA
Kuching
Singapore
INDONESIA
Jakarta

MADAGASCAR
MAURITIUS

INDIAN OCEAN

TIMOR SEA

AUSTRALIA

Longitude East of Greenwich

The Maldivian dhoani is a decorative, durable craft designed for efficient shallow water sailing.

Atlas of the Maldives
Introduction

The marvellous and once mysterious Maldive Islands, remain just as intriguing as ever and continue to divulge their secrets with every passing year. Atlas of the Maldives illustrates the diversity of geographical, historical and cultural features that make up this Indian Ocean Archipelago, as well as making island identification and location easier. It includes underwater maps of Protected Marine Areas as well as navigation lights, shipwrecks, and a comprehensive island index.

As the resorts continue to expand into the outer atolls, they provide the basis for change, bringing added interest to the regions they serve. The atoll charts include resorts and the location of proposed resorts. In recognising the importance of island names to the history of the Maldives, traditional island names are included in brackets when a resort changes the island's name.

New harbours and reclamation of land are constantly changing the shape of islands. Some maps of key islands have been included, revealing in considerable detail, some of these changes. When complemented with photos, Atlas of the Maldives illustrates the lifestyle, development aspirations and resources of the people.

Islands of Kaafu with Velassaru in the foreground.

Most importantly, this atlas is designed to be an informative reference for travelling around the atolls. Having a clear understanding of the island names and their locations, as well as knowing some of the main features, will undoubtedly lead to a more rewarding travel experience.

ATOLLS OF THE MALDIVES

In the English dictionary, an 'atoll' is defined as "a ring-shaped coral reef and small island, enclosing a lagoon and surrounded by open sea." Within this definition, there are many hundreds of atolls in the Maldives. In broader terms these 'micro' atolls make up 25 distinct geographical atoll formations. They are spread in a north – south direction over a distance of 868 km between latitude 7°6'30"N and 0°42'30"S.

The British Admiralty, in their comprehensive bathymetric survey of the islands in 1834-36, defined where these atoll boundaries were and named each atoll according to local names. Open seas or deep channels with a depth of more than 200 metres were considered separate atolls. There are 25 distinct atolls but if Kuda Kanduolhi - a 200 metre deep channel that divides South Maalhosmadulu Atoll - is considered an atoll division, then the total number of atolls is 26. The largest atoll, Huvadhoo, is 65 km wide and 82 km long, while Thoddoo, the smallest, is about 1.8 km in diameter. Depths within the atolls usually vary between 30 to 50 metres but in some places, such as Huvadhoo Atoll, depths may reach up to 90 metres.

The word "atoll" is derived from the Maldivian word "atholu", the only Maldivian word to have found it's way into the English dictionary. An atholu is an administrative region that in some parts of the Maldives, takes in more or less of these distinctly separate geographical coral reef formations. From the viewpoint of a boatman, sailing the length of the Maldives, most of the islands in the south are clearly part of distinctly separate atolls. In the north, however, many islands appear more isolated and the atoll boundaries appear less defined.

ADMINISTRATIVE REGIONS

The 25 atolls are divided into 21 administrative regions. Malé, the capital, is an entity in itself and makes up the 21st region. These administrative regions are named after the letters of the Maldivian alphabet and begin with "Haa", in the north to "Seenu", in the south. Some administrative regions are divided into north (alifu)/south (dhaalu) zones. With so many islands in the Maldives - many with the same name - islands are usually identified by adding a prefix to the island name with the abbreviated letters of the administrative region in which it lies. For instance, there are two islands with the name Govvaafushi.

HA Govvaafushi is in Haa Alifu while LH Govvaafushi is in Lhaviyani. Abbreviations for the regions are as follows: HA for Haa Alifu, HD for Haa Dhaalu, SH for Shaviyani, N for Noonu, RA for Raa, BA for Baa, LH for Lhaviyani, KA for Kaafu, AA for Alifu Alifu, AD for Alifu Dhaalu, FA for Faafu, DH for Dhaalu, ME for Meemu, TH for Thaa, LA for Laamu, GA for Gaafu Alifu, VA for Vaavu, GD for Gaafu Dhaalu, GN for Gnaviyani and SE for Seenu.

ISLANDS OF THE MALDIVES

There are an estimated 1190 islands in the Maldives with some form of vegetation on them, whether grass, bushes, or trees. Of this total, there are 200 inhabited islands and 990 uninhabited. This total figure can change from year to year as islands are continually being eroded and washed away, while others are being formed. Some islands, such as Thilafushi and Hulhumalé have been reclaimed. At a height of three metres, Hulhumalé is considered to be the highest island in the Maldives.

The number of 'inhabited' islands does not refer to the actual number of islands, but the administrative areas of those islands. For instance, Malé, the capital of the Maldives, includes Villingili and Hulhulmalé within it's administrative boundaries and all three are considered as 'one' island. In Seenu Atoll, Maradhoo and Maradhoo-Feydhoo are on the same geographical island but are considered as two separate 'islands'. The same applies to Meedhoo and Hulhudhoo, which have separate populations, but are on the same island. Other islands, like GD Fares and GD Maathoda have been joined together by land reclamation, but are still considered as separate islands.

Even though many uninhabited islands are unoccupied and in a natural state, many have some type of industry, whether it be agricultural or storage, and are clearly occupied at certain times, if not all the time. Tourist resorts are also defined as being 'uninhabited'.

TOURISM

The Maldives has a yearly temperature range from 25° C to 32°C and two monsoon seasons, the NE Monsoon from December to April and the SW Monsoon, from May to November. The warm, tropical climate attracts divers and travellers from around the world to 88 resorts and 117 safari vessels. In addition, there are 24 guest houses and 9 hotels. Another 39 resorts are either proposed or under construction and within two years there will be resorts in every atoll of the Maldives. A further two regional airports at LH Madivaru and AD Maamigili are proposed to cater for the extra numbers. In the south, the International airport at Gan, Addu Atoll, will open up the southern region and serve as its hub.

POPULATION

The island population figures shown on the atoll maps are the registered populations of the islands based on the June 2003 survey. These population statistics have changed since the 2004 Tsunami and because some island populations are still being relocated, these statistics had not been finalised at the time of printing. The total population of the Maldives in 2003/04 was 294,356. Census figures show the total population on an island at any given time and are not an accurate reflection of that island's registered population. For instance, Malé's registered population in 2003 was 46,274 people, yet the census figure was 76,350. This figure is now considerably higher. Some islands are in the process of change. For instance, on SH Maakadoodhoo, (pop 1166) the entire population is being moved to SH Milandhoo, about 6 kms to the north, because the current island does not offer a good harbour. About half the population has been moved, and when the transition is complete, SH Maakadoodhoo will become uninhabited. In the mean time, the registered population figures show SH Maakadoodhoo as being the inhabited island. Other population changes have resulted because of the Tsunami (see page 13).

NAVIGATION

The charts contained within this book are not designed for navigation and should not be used for such purposes. The latest British Admiralty surveys in WGS 84 datum, have been corrected for use with the Global Positioning System (GPS) and can be used in either chart or digital formats. However, the charts in this book can be used as an aid to navigation. They were compiled by using a combination of US satellite charts from 1986, British Admiralty Charts, black and white aerial transect survey photos from the 1960's and local knowledge from underwater diving surveys. Other features from various government departments and private organizations have been added to complement the charts.

The most useful visual reference while travelling around by boat are the communication towers. They are located throughout the atolls and they should all have a light at the top of the tower, making them visible at night. Towers less than 67m have a light at the top only. Tower heights exceeding that have a light at an intermediate height of 45m. At Foammulah, tower lights are at 3 different stages (45m, 90m & 120m). The tower at GD Gadhdhoo is of the same height and has lights at similar heights. In 2002 and 2003, 14 new towers 45m in height were erected within the atolls. In 2005/2006 a second communications company began operations and a further 146 towers were erected.

LIGHTS

Since the year 2000, a program to establish navigation/marker lights in the atolls has been carried out by the Ministry of Transport & Civil Aviation. This major project involves identifying reefs, installing lights and marking their positions to enable safer, nighttime navigation for local vessels. For the first time, these lights are shown on Maldives charts. There are 85 lights with a 12-mile radius that have been constructed around the perimeter of the atolls and at the entrance to major shipping channels. A further 146 lights with a 2 mile radius have been established within the atolls to identify prominent reefs along the major trading routes. Along with the lights, an extra 63 reefs and channel names were added to the charts, bringing new identity to otherwise unnamed areas. The positions of all lights have been checked with the Ministry of Transport and Civil Aviation, however, caution should be exercised in relying on them. The 2 mile lights are designed for use by local boat captains only and new lights are constantly being added, some may be temporarily disabled, and others may even be moved. In addition, a further 30 MIFCO (Maldives Industrial Fisheries Company Ltd) lights have been included on the major trading routes in Huvadhoo Atoll.

REGIONAL DEVELOPMENT ISLANDS

A number of islands are being developed to provide all public conveniences and to act as hubs for island population growth. Facilities such as schools, hospitals and harbours are being directed to these islands as well as other investments to encourage employment. Land reclamation on some islands will provide more space for housing. These islands include HD Kulhudhuffushi, LH Naifaru, LA Fonadhoo-Gan, GN Foammulah, SE Hithadhoo.

FISHING ISLANDS

Fishing has traditionally been carried out by every inhabited island of the Maldives, but as the commercial industry has grown, so too have certain islands become hubs for the expanding fleets of vessels. There are 54 major fishing islands throughout the Maldives. They have been identified by the amount of fish-mainly tuna-caught over a three-year period from the year 2000. Employment at these islands is

The island of Rasfari, Kaafu, showing its communication tower, one of many scattered around the atolls.

A 12 Mile Light, Velassaru Faru. Kaafu

mostly based around fishing. From this total, a further 20 islands are identified as the major fish catching islands in the Maldives. These islands have been shown on the charts. There are currently four fishing zones within the Maldives. Each zone has two fishing operators that are based at different island ports. These islands include facilities for storing fish, whether they are frozen, chilled or live. The operators send collector vessels to outlying islands in their zone that specialise in catching and landing fish.

There are currently three fish processing islands in the Maldives. LH Felivaru has a fish canning factory and GA Kooddoo and LA Mundoo are cold storage and fish processing plants. A further three cold storage and fish processing plants are proposed for HA Huvahandhoo, SH Keekimini and TH Fonaddoo. KA Kanduoiygiri is a fresh chilled plant for processing larger fish like Yellow fin tuna into steaks.

FADS

There are currently 43 FADS (Fish Aggregating Devices) located in deep water around the outside of the Maldives. They mostly occur between 12 to 15 nautical miles off the coast and are fastened with mooring lines to concrete blocks at about 3000 to 4000 metres. Their position, however, is not always fixed. It varies with a radius of about one kilometre as the buoy swings on its axis. Buoys are sometimes cut or lost in heavy seas and replaced by another buoy in a different position. Also, fishermen sometimes request that the buoy be moved to other areas. For this reason, their positions have not been included on the charts. Fish, in particular tuna, are attracted to these floating devices and fishermen use them for pole and line fishing. The FADS are distributed evenly around every atoll. There are two types and those with lights and antennas are located at the extremities of the atolls as indicators to shipping.

AGRICULTURAL ISLANDS

Some inhabited and uninhabited islands are recognised as being major contributors to agricultural production in the Maldives. Some islands specialize in a particular fruit, vegetable or crop. AA Thoddoo, for instance, specializes in watermelons and chillies, SH Feevah in bananas and mango, HA Kelaa in vegetables like tomatoes and beans, as well as fruits such as banana and papaya, HD Vaikaradhoo in cereals like millet and sorghum, GD Vaadhoo and GN Gnaviyani in yams and taro, HD Finey in pumpkins and luffa, and KA

Kaashidhoo in coconuts, chillies and bananas. SH Goidhoo is more general while GA Nilandhoo is more seasonal and tends to produce crops when the fishing is not as good, for instance in the SW Monsoon months of June and July, or before Ramadan. Other islands such as HD Nolhivaramu and ME Kolhuvaariyaafushi have only recently, in the past five years or so, become more productive in various cash crops. Other major producing islands such as LA Isdhoo, LA Kalaidhoo and GD Hoadedhdhoo, provide much of the produce for their atolls. GD Hoadedhdhoo even has a daily ferry to the capital Thinadhoo.

PROTECTED MARINE AREAS

On World Environment Day, June 5, 1995, the Government of the Maldives announced the establishment of 15 Protected Marine Areas within the major tourist atolls. A further nine areas were identified in 1999. These locations are shown on the charts and detailed underwater maps of these sites have been included. They are areas recognized for their diversity, significance or proximity to resorts and are exceptional diving areas. For these sites to be effectively protected, they need recognition and policing against marauding fishermen.

The island of Guraidhoo, Kaafu and Guraidhoo Kandu, a Protected Marine Area.

ISLAND CHANGES FOLLOWING 2004 TSUNAMI.

The tsunami of December 26th, 2004 affected every island in the Maldives - some more than others - and highlighted the economic and environmental vulnerability of the country. Following the tsunami, the government initiated a voluntary migration incentive scheme to reduce the number of inhabited islands and consolidate isolated settlements.

Most of the islands destroyed by the tsunami had little or no coastal protection and as part of the ongoing atoll development strategy, the concept of tsunami "safe islands" is being implemented.

The idea of safe islands is to extend the population consolidation approach to establishing building and construction codes to provide safe areas where basic services in an emergency, particularly health, communication, transport and a buffer stock of food and water, can be provided. The features of safe islands are improved coastal protection, communication and transport facilities, housing, infrastructure, social services and adequate capacity and preparedness to manage emergencies and disasters.

The basis for selection of safe islands was size, availability of existing government offices and availability of free space to serve as host islands for relocating population.

Above and top right: The tsunami caused significant damage to many islands.

The islands relocated under the tsunami reconstruction development program are:
1. RA Kandholhudhoo.
   People relocated to RA Dhuvaafaru.
2. ME Madifushi.
   People relocated to AD Maamigili
3. DH Gemendhoo.
   People relocated to DH Kudahuvadhoo

The islands relocated under the population and development consolidation policy are:
1. HA Berimmadhoo.
   People relocated to HA Huvarafushi
2. SH Maakandoodhoo.
   People relocated to SH Milandhoo.

The islands to be relocated under the population and development consolidation policy are:
1. GA Dhiyadhoo.
   People relocated to GA Gemanafushi, GA Kodey and LA Gan.
2. HA Hathifushi.
   People relocated to HA Huvarafushi or HD Nolhivaranfaru.
3. HD Faridhoo, HD Kuburudhoo, HD Maavaidhoo.
   People relocated to HD Nolhivaranfaru.
4. BA Fehendhoo.
   People relocated to BA Goidhoo.

The 14 "safe islands" selected are:		The "most Tsunami affected" islands are:	
HD Nolhivaranfaru	HD Kulhuduffushi	KA Dhiffushi	DH Kudahuvadhoo
SH Funadhoo	RA Dhuvaafaru	DH Ribudhoo	DH Gemendhoo
ME Muli	DH Kudahuvadhoo	DH Vaanee	TH Vilufushi
KA Thulusdhoo	TH Thimarafushi	TH Madifushi	LA Gan
TH Vilufushi	LA Gan	LA Mundhoo	LA Kalhaidhoo
LH Hinnavaru	GA Villingili	LA Maabaidhoo	RA Kandhdhudhoo
GD Thinadhoo	SE Gan-Hithadhoo	ME Madifushi	ME Kolhufushi

Malé

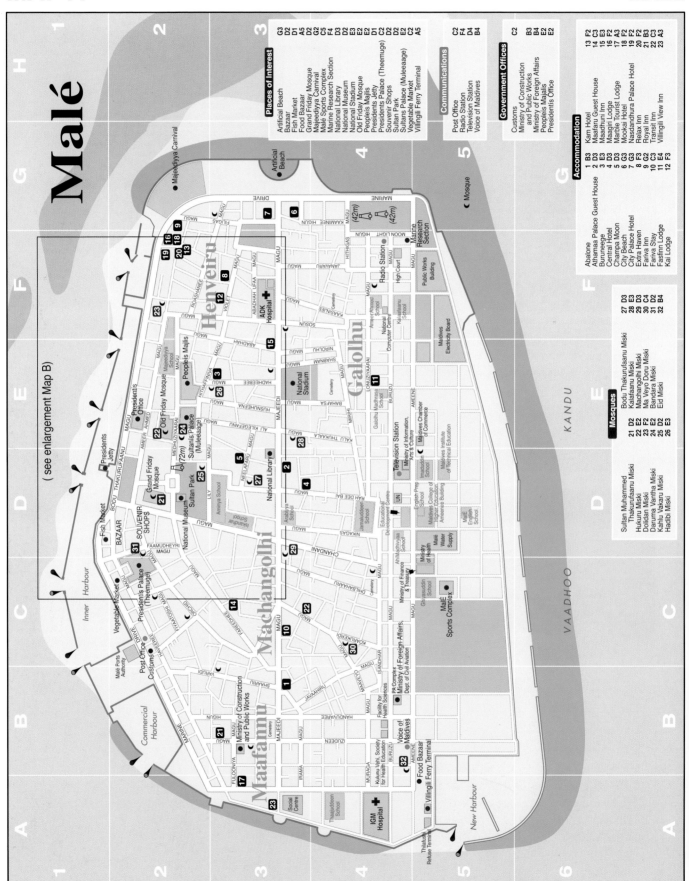

(see enlargement Map B)

Places of Interest

Artificial Beach	G3
Bazaar	D2
Fish Market	D1
Food Bazaar	A5
Grand Friday Mosque	D2
Majeediyya Carnival	G2
Malé Sports Complex	C5
Marine Research Section	F4
National Library	D3
National Museum	D2
National Stadium	E3
Old Friday Mosque	E2
Peoples Majlis	E2
Presidents Jetty	D1
Presidents Palace (Theemuge)	C2
Souvenir Shops	D2
Sultan Park	E2
Sultans Palace (Muleeaage)	E2
Vegetable Market	C2
Villingili Ferry Terminal	A5

Communications

Post Office	C2
Radio Station	F4
Television Station	D4
Voice of Maldives	B4

Government Offices

Customs	C2
Ministry of Construction and Public Works	B3
Ministry of Foreign Affairs	B4
Peoples Majalis	E2
Presidents Office	E2

Accommodation

Abalone	13	F2
Athamaa Palace Guest House	14	C3
Buruneege	15	F2
Central Hotel	16	F2
Champa Moon	17	A3
City Beach	18	F2
City Palace Hotel	19	F2
Extra Haven	20	F2
Fariva Inn	21	B3
Fariva Stay	22	C3
Fasfim Lodge	23	A3
Kai Lodge		
Kam Hotel	1	B3
Maafaru Guest House	2	D3
Maadhuni Inn	3	D3
Maagiri Lodge	4	D3
Marble Tourist Lodge	5	D3
Mookai Hotel	6	G3
Nasdandhura Palace Hotel	7	G3
Relax Inn	8	F3
Royal Inn	9	G2
Transit Inn	10	C3
Villingili View Inn	11	E4
	12	F2

Mosques

Sultan Muhammed Thakurufaanu Miski	21	D2
Hukuru Miski	22	E2
Dolidan Miski	23	F2
Daruma Vantha Miski	24	E2
Kahlu Vakaru Miski	25	D2
Hadibi Miski	26	E3
Bodu Thakurufaanu Miski	27	D3
Kalafaanu Miski	28	E3
Machangolhi Miski	29	D3
Ma Veyo Doru Miski	30	D2
Bandara Miski	31	D2
Eid Miski	32	B4

Satellite image of Malé taken December 2003.

HISTORY OF THE MALDIVES

The archaeological ruins of temples, old mosques, shipwrecks, forts and memorials that remain on many islands form a snapshot of an intriguing history of the Maldives. Many artefacts have been found and are housed at the National Museum in Malé. Others remain buried and occasionally see the light of day, supporting ongoing research being carried out at the Centre for Linguistic and Historical Research, Malé.

1. The old fort in Malé, The Akoatey Buruzu, early 1900's. 2. Old Mosque on Gnaviyani. 3. British War Memorial, Seenu.
4. The old mosque on Kolhufushi in Meemu was badly damaged in the 2004 Tsunami. 5. Stonework from the remains of 'Nilandhoo Foamathi' in Faafu. 6. A holy tomb or 'Ziyaarai' on Vaadhoo in Gaafu Dhaalu.

AIRPORTS AND HARBOURS OF THE MALDIVES

The Malé International Airport (Hulhule) is located in the middle of the Maldives and is connected by a 20 minute ferry service to the capital Malé. The airport – which was once two islands joined together in 1968 - includes a seaplane terminal on the east side of the island that shuttles passengers to their respective resorts. A second International Airport is located at Gan in Addu Atoll. There are three regional airports, Hanimadhoo, Kadhdhoo, and Kaadedhdhoo with a fourth, Madivaru, planned to open in Faadhippolhu Atoll in late 2007. Another regional airport is planned for Maamigili, in South Ari Atoll.

1. The regional airport of Hanimaadhoo in Haa Dhaalu 2. Malé harbour. 3. The new Malé harbour 4. Hulhule Airport, Kaafu. 5. Gan Airport, Seenu. 6. The regional airport of Kaadedhdhoo, Gaafu Dhaalu. 7. The harbour at Muli, Meemu, damaged during the Tsunami.

SHIPWRECKS

The Maldives Archipelago lies across the direct sea route between Southern Arabia, Sri Lanka and the Far East and was once a formidable barrier to shipping in the region. Many ships have run aground and remain on the reefs, often unidentified. Others are reported to have been wrecked but cannot be located. Some have been scuttled. A list of shipwrecks compiled by the Centre for Linguistic and Historical Research and other wrecks - located and reported by divers - are shown on the reefs where found. When a wreck is known to exist on a reef but has not been identified, it often takes on the name of the reef on which it lies. Other ships known to have been wrecked but cannot be located, are included on the charts with their name and date (when known) positioned *off* the reef in the general area they were reported lost. G.P.S. positions of all wrecks are approximate positions, and are for reference only.

1. The Halavelli wreck, 1991. Alifu Alifu. 2. The Skipjack 11, 1985. Lhaviyani. 3. The Erlangen, 1894. Gaafaru, Kaafu. 4. The Lady Christine, April 16, 1974. Gaafaru, Kaafu. 5. The anchor of the SS Sea Gull, 1879. Gaafaru, Kaafu.

6. The 'Shipyard' in Felivaru Kandu is one of the main diving attractions in Lhaviyani Atoll. 7. Kuda Giri Wreck, Kaafu. 8. The Al Kareem was scuttled on the north side of Ranveli Village, Alifu Alifu, 2000 9. The Maldive Victory, Feb 13, 1981. Kaafu. 10. Propeller of the British Loyalty, Seenu. 11. Remains of a World War II submarine net, Viligili Kandu, Seenu. 12. The anchor of the Dutch East Indiaman, Ravestein, May 9, 1726. Alifu Alifu. 13. The Rayvilla, 1979. Meemu.

INHABITED ISLANDS
OF THE MALDIVES

Many inhabited islands are very isolated and rarely visited by the tourist population. In the future this may change as new resorts are developed in the outer atolls. Communications have brought improved contact between the islands and now local residents can speak to relatives on islands they may never visit or have never seen.

1. The island of Foammulah, Gnaviyani, showing the 120 meter communications tower. 2. Rasdhoo in foreground and Kuramathi, Alifu Alifu.
3. Dharavandhoo, Baa. 4. Nilandhoo, Faafu. 5. Thulusdhoo, Kaafu. 6. The island of Hanghghaameedhoo and Uthuru Athafaru reef, Alifu Alifu.
7. The island of Naalaafushi looking towards Muli, Meemu.

UNINHABITED ISLANDS OF THE MALDIVES

An estimated 990 uninhabited islands lay scattered throughout the Maldives archipelago. Many of these islands have resorts or building structures on them or may be leased for agricultural purposes. Others may have previously been inhabited but in most cases the islands are in a pristine state and remain undisturbed. Some have a gap in the outer reef allowing access to a shallow water lagoon but most remain inaccessible to all but the most shallow drafted vessels.

1. Kuda Bandos, Kaafu. 2. The inner lagoon of Hudhufushi, Lhaviyani, is a nursery for baby sharks. 3. Kudadhoo, Lhaviyani.
4. Funamauddoo, Gaafu Alifu. 5. Hurasdhoo, Alifu Dhaalu. 6. The island of Thanburudhoo, Kaafu, with Girifushi in the background.

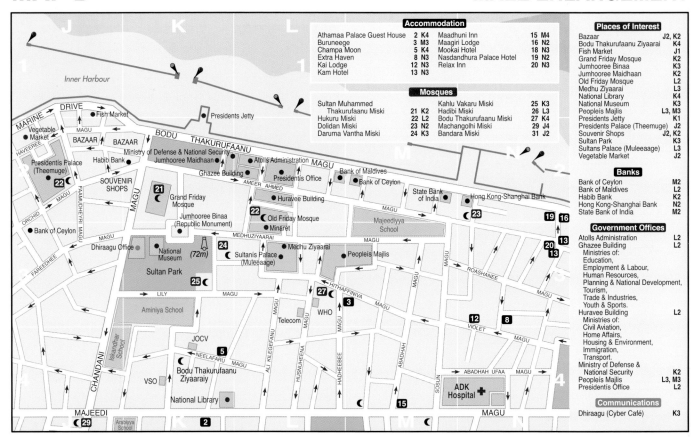

Accommodation		
Athamaa Palace Guest House	2	K4
Buruneege	3	M3
Champa Moon	5	K4
Extra Haven	8	N3
Kai Lodge	12	N3
Kam Hotel	13	N3
Maadhuni Inn	15	M4
Maagiri Lodge	16	N2
Mookai Hotel	18	N3
Nasdandhura Palace Hotel	19	N2
Relax Inn	20	N3

Mosques		
Sultan Muhammed Thakurufaanu Miski	21	K2
Hukuru Miski	22	L2
Dolidan Miski	23	N2
Daruma Vantha Miski	24	K3
Kahlu Vakaru Miski	25	K3
Hadibi Miski	26	L3
Bodu Thakurufaanu Miski	27	K4
Machangolhi Miski	29	J4
Bandara Miski	31	J2

Places of Interest	
Bazaar	J2, K2
Bodu Thakurufaanu Ziyaarai	K4
Fish Market	J1
Grand Friday Mosque	K2
Jumhooree Binaa	K3
Jumhooree Maidhaan	K2
Old Friday Mosque	L2
Medhu Ziyaarai	L3
National Library	K4
National Museum	K3
Peopleís Majlis	L3, M3
Presidents Jetty	K1
Presidents Palace (Theemuge)	J2
Souvenir Shops	J2, K2
Sultan Park	K3
Sultans Palace (Muleeaage)	L3
Vegetable Market	J2

Banks	
Bank of Ceylon	M2
Bank of Maldives	L2
Habib Bank	L2
Hong Kong-Shanghai Bank	N2
State Bank of India	M2

Government Offices	
Atolls Administration	L2
Ghazee Building	L2
Ministries of: Education, Employment & Labour, Human Resources, Planning & National Development, Tourism, Trade & Industries, Youth & Sports.	
Huravee Building	L2
Ministries of: Civil Aviation, Home Affairs, Housing & Environment, Immigration, Transport.	
Ministry of Defense & National Security	K2
Peopleís Majlis	L3, M3
Presidentís Office	L2

Communications	
Dhiraagu (Cyber Café)	K3

1. Jumhooree Maidhaan. The National flag of the Maldives. **2.** Minaret, Old Friday Mosque, built 1675 by Sultan Iskander I. **3.** Kalhu Vakaru Miski. One of the oldest mosques in Malé. **4.** Fish Market. **5.** Medhu Ziyarat, the last resting place of the saint, Abul Barakat, who converted the Maldives to Islam. **6.** Vegetable market.

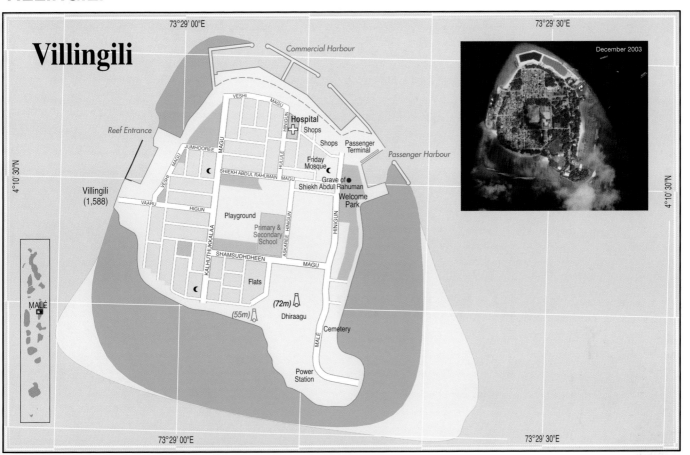

7. The minaret of the main mosque in Malé, the Sultan Muhammed Thakurufaanu Miski. 8. The President's Palace, Theemuge. 9. The Sultan's Palace, Muleeaage, the former residence of Sultan's and President's. 10. Bodu Thakurufaanu Ziyaarai. Tomb of the leader who led a rebellion that defeated the Portuguese in 1558. 11. The People's Majlis or Parliment building, the meeting place of the legislative body of the government. 12. Old Friday Mosque or Hukuru Miski, built in 1656, was constructed on the site of the first mosque built in Malé.

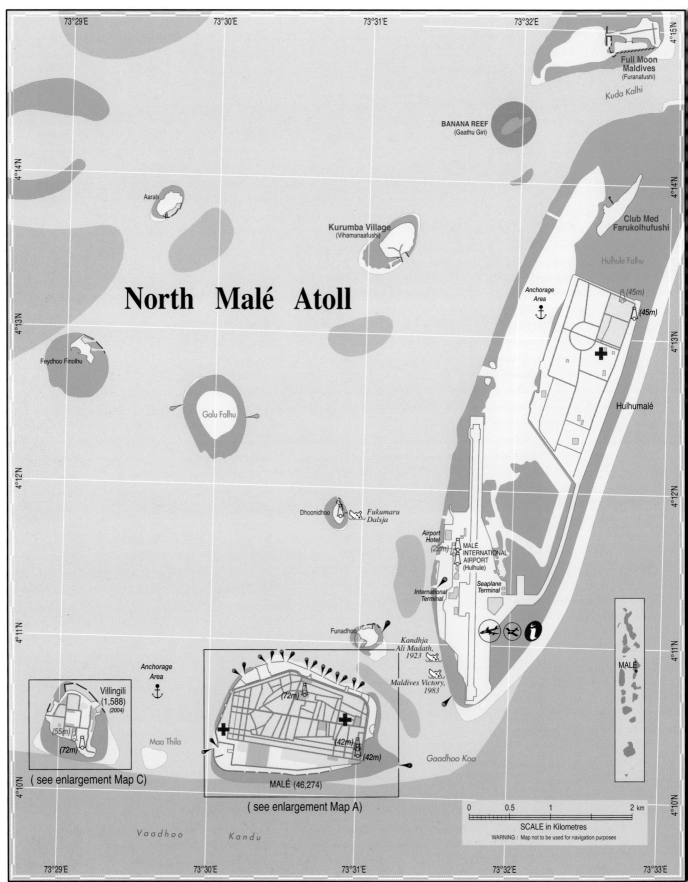

Full Moon Maldives
(Furanafushi)

Kuda Kalhi

BANANA REEF
(Gaathu Giri)

4°15'N

4°14'N

Aarah

Kurumba Village
(Vihamanaafushi)

Club Med Farukolhufushi

4°14'N

Hulhule Falhu

North Malé Atoll

Anchorage Area

4°13'N

(45m)

(45m)

Feydhoo Finolhu

4°13'N

Hulhumalé

Galu Falhu

4°12'N

4°12'N

Dhoonidhoo

Fukumaru Dalsja

Airport Hotel (22m)

MALÉ INTERNATIONAL AIRPORT (Hulhule)

4°11'N

Funadhoo

International Terminal

Seaplane Terminal

Kandhja Ali Madath, 1923

4°11'N

Anchorage Area

Villingili
(1,588)
(2004)

Maldives Victory, 1983

MALÉ

(55m)

(72m)

(72m)

Maa Thila

(42m)

(42m)

(42m)

Gaadhoo Koa

(see enlargement Map C)

MALÉ (46,274)

4°10'N

4°10'N

(see enlargement Map A)

Vaadhoo   Kandu

0	0.5	1	2 km

SCALE in Kilometres

WARNING : Map not to be used for navigation purposes

73°29'E   73°30'E   73°31'E   73°32'E   73°33'E

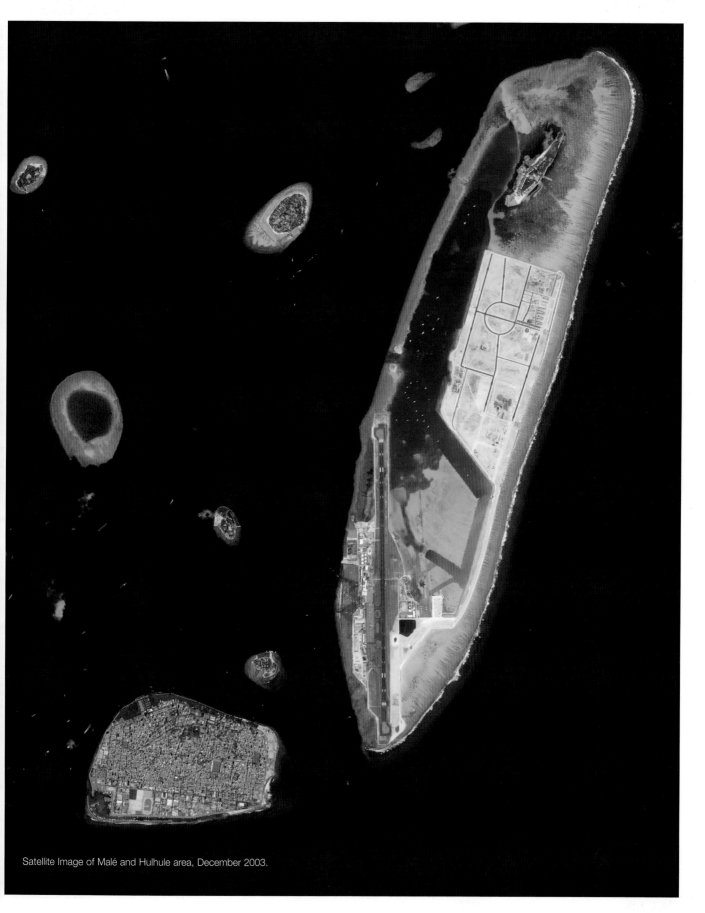

Satellite Image of Malé and Hulhule area, December 2003.

MAP 1

HAA ALIFU

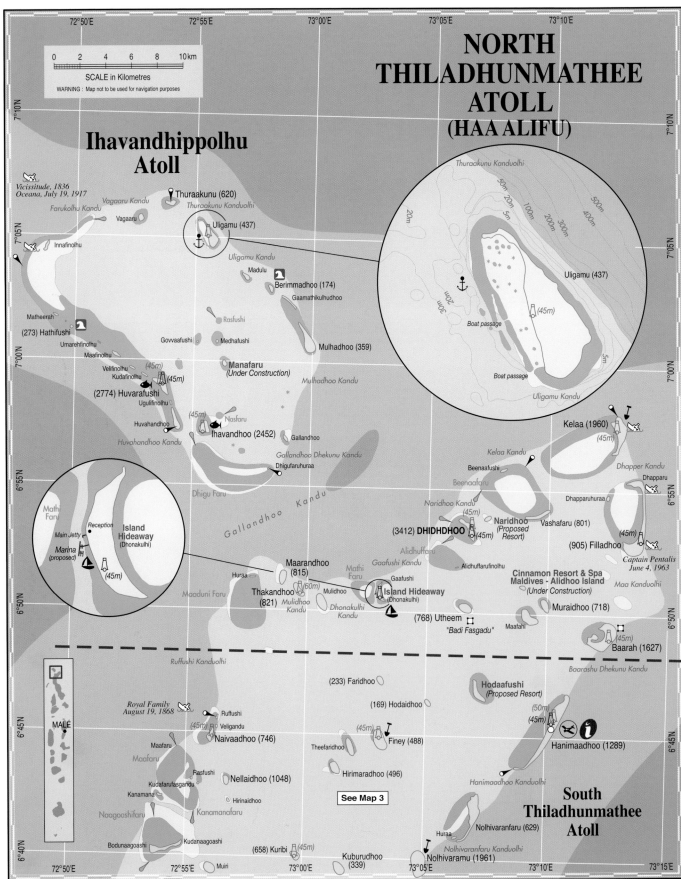

NORTH THILADHUNMATHEE ATOLL (HAA ALIFU)

Ihavandhippolhu Atoll

Vicissitude, 1836
Oceana, July 19, 1917

Vagaaru Kandu

Vagaaru

Innafinolhu

Farukolhu Kandu

Matheerah

(273) Hathifushi

Umarehfinolhu

Maafinolhu

Velifinolhu
Kudafinolhu *(45m)*

(2774) Huvarafushi

Ugulifinolhu

Huvahandhoo *(45m)*

Nasfaru

Ihavandhoo (2452)

Gallandhoo

Huvahandhoo Kandu

Thuraakunu (620)

Thuraakunu Kanduolhi

Uligamu (437)

Uligamu Kandu

Madulu

Berimmadhoo (174)

Gaamathikulhudhoo

Rasfushi

Govvaafushi   Medhafushi

Manafaru
(Under Construction)

Mulhadhoo (359)

Mulhadhoo Kandu

Thuraakunu Kanduolhi

50m 20m 5m 100m 200m 300m 400m 500m

20m

Uligamu (437)

30m 20m

5m

Boat passage

Boat passage

Uligamu Kandu

Dhigufaruhuraa

Gallandhoo Dhekunu Kandu

Gallandhoo Kandu

Dhigu Faru

Mathi Faru

Reception

Main Jetty

Marina
(proposed)

Island Hideaway
(Dhonakulhi)

(45m)

Huraa

Maarandhoo
(815)

Thakandhoo
(821)

Mulidhoo

Mathi Faru

Gaafushi

Island Hideaway
(Dhonakulhi)

Mulidhoo Kandu

Dhonakulhi Kandu

Gaafushi Kandu

Alidhuffaru

Alidhuffarufinolhu

(768) Utheem
"Badi Fasgadu"

Maafahi

Kelaa (1960)

(45m)

Beenaafushi

Beenaafaru

Naridhoo Kandu

(45m)

(3412) DHIDHDHOO

(45m)

Naridhoo
(Proposed Resort)

Vashafaru (801)

Dhapper Kandu

Dhappuru

Dhapparuhuraa

(45m)

(905) Filladhoo

Captain Pentalis
June 4, 1963

Cinnamon Resort & Spa
Maldives - Alidhoo Island
(Under Construction)

Muraidhoo (718)

Maa Kanduolhi

(45m)

Baarah (1627)

Ruffushi Kanduolhi

Baarashu Dhekunu Kandu

(233) Faridhoo

(169) Hodaidhoo

Hodaafushi
(Proposed Resort)

(50m)

(45m)

Royal Family
August 19, 1868

Ruffushi

(45m) Veligandu

Maafaru

Naivaadhoo (746)

MALÉ

Theefaridhoo

(45m)

Finey (488)

Hanimaadhoo (1289)

Rasfushi

Nellaidhoo (1048)

Kudafarufasgandu

Kanamana

Hirinaidhoo

Hirimaradhoo (496)

See Map 3

Hanimaadhoo Kanduolhi

South Thiladhunmathee Atoll

Naagoashifaru

Kanamanafaru

Bodunaagoashi

Kudanaagoashi

(658) Kuribi *(45m)*

Muiri

Kuburudhoo
(339)

Nolhivaramu (1961)

Nolhivaranfaru Kanduolhi

Huraa

Nolhivaranfaru (629)

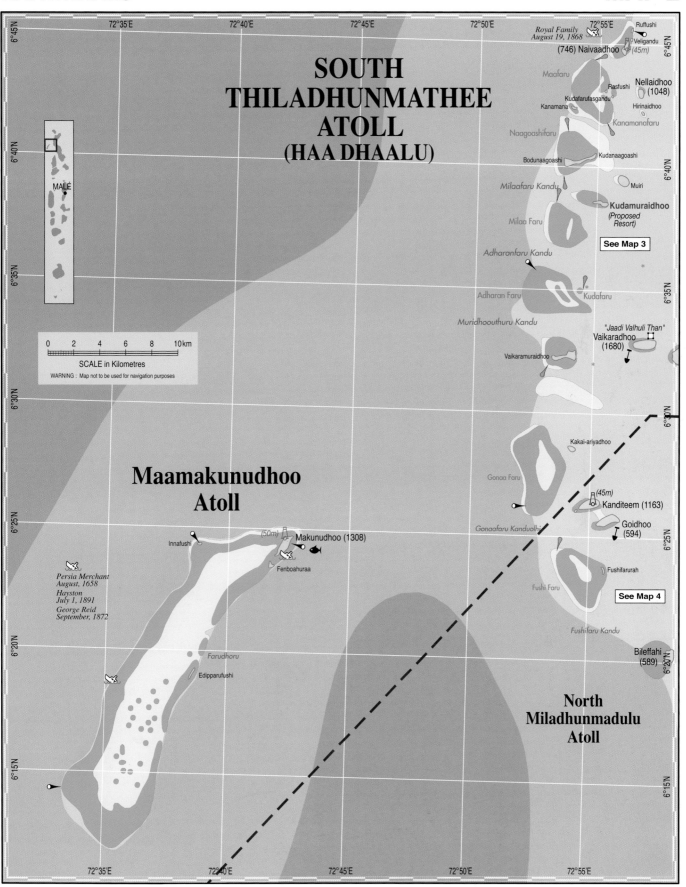

SOUTH THILADHUNMATHEE ATOLL (HAA DHAALU)

Royal Family August 19, 1868

Ruffushi

Veligandu *(45m)*

(746) Naivaadhoo

Maafaru

Rasfushi

Nellaidhoo (1048)

Kudafarufasgandu

Kanamana

Hirinaidhoo

Kanamanafaru

Naagoashifaru

Kudanaagoashi

Bodunaagoashi

Muiri

Milaafaru Kandu

Kudamuraidhoo

(Proposed Resort)

Milaa Faru

See Map 3

Adharanfaru Kandu

Adharan Faru

Kudafaru

Muridhoouthuru Kandu

"Jaadi Valhuli Than"

Vaikaradhoo (1680)

Vaikaramuraidhoo

MALÉ

Maamakunudhoo Atoll

Kakai-ariyadhoo

Gonaa Faru

(45m)

Kanditeem (1163)

Goidhoo (594)

Gonaafaru Kanduolhi

(50m)

Innafushi

Makunudhoo (1308)

Fushifarurah

Fenboahuraa

Fushi Faru

See Map 4

Persia Merchant August, 1658

Hayston July 1, 1891

George Reid September, 1872

Fushifaru Kandu

Farudhoru

Bileffahi (589)

Edipparufushi

North Miladhunmadulu Atoll

0 2 4 6 8 10km

SCALE in Kilometres

WARNING : Map not to be used for navigation purposes

MAP 3

HAA DHAALU

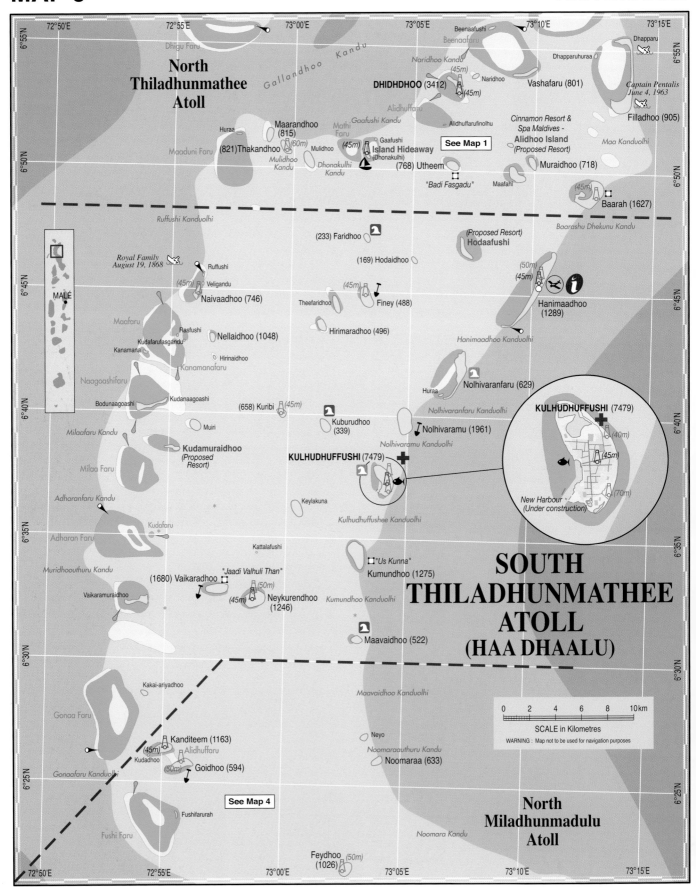

North
Thiladhunmathee
Atoll

Dhigu Faru

Gallandhoo Kandu

Beenaafushi
Beenaafaru

Dhapparu

Dhapparuhuraa

Naridhoo Kandu
(45m)

Naridhoo

Vashafaru (801)

Captain Pentalis
June 4, 1963

DHIDHDHOO (3412)
(45m)

Alidhuffaru

Filladhoo (905)

Gaafushi Kandu

Cinnamon Resort &
Spa Maldives -
Alidhoo Island
(Proposed Resort)

Maa Kanduolhi

Huraa

Maarandhoo
(815)

Mathi
Faru

Alidhuffarufinolhu

(821)Thakandhoo
(60m)

Mulidhoo

Gaafushi

Maaduni Faru
Mulidhoo
Kandu

(45m)
Island Hideaway
(Dhonakulhi)

Muraidhoo (718)

Dhonakulhi
Kandu

(768) Utheem

"Badi Fasgadu"

Maafahi

Baarah (1627)
(45m)

Ruffushi Kanduolhi

Baarashu Dhekunu Kandu

(233) Faridhoo

(Proposed Resort)
Hodaafushi

Royal Family
August 19, 1868

Ruffushi

(169) Hodaidhoo

(50m)

MALÉ

(45m)
Veligandu

(45m)

(45m)

Naivaadhoo (746)

Theefaridhoo

Finey (488)

Hanimaadhoo
(1289)

Maafaru

Rasfushi

Nellaidhoo (1048)

Hirimaradhoo (496)

Kudafarulasgandu

Hirinaidhoo

Hanimaadhoo Kanduolhi

Kanamana

Kanamanafaru

Naagoashifaru

Huraa

Nolhivaranfaru (629)

KULHUDHUFFUSHI (7479)

Bodunaagoashi

Kudanaagoashi

(658) Kuribi
(45m)

Nolhivaranfaru Kanduolhi

(40m)

Muiri

Kuburudhoo
(339)

Nolhivaramu (1961)

(45m)

Milaafaru Kandu

Nolhivaramu Kanduolhi

Kudamuraidhoo
(Proposed
Resort)

KULHUDHUFFUSHI (7479)

(45m)

Milaa Faru

Adharanfaru Kandu

Keylakuna

New Harbour
(Under construction)

(70m)

Adharan Faru

Kudafaru

Kulhudhuffushee Kanduolhi

*

Muridhoouthuru Kandu

*

Kattalafushi

"Us Kunna"

SOUTH
THILADHUNMATHEE
ATOLL
(HAA DHAALU)

(1680) Vaikaradhoo

"Jaadi Valhuli Than"

Kumundhoo (1275)

(50m)

Vaikaramuraidhoo

Neykurendhoo
(1246)

Kumundhoo Kanduolhi

(45m)

*

Maavaidhoo (522)

Maavaidhoo Kanduolhi

Kakai-ariyadhoo

Gonaa Faru

Neyo

Noomaraauthuru Kandu

Kanditeem (1163)

Noomaraa (633)

(45m)
Alidhuffaru

Kudadhoo

Goidhoo (594)

(50m)

0   2   4   6   8   10km

SCALE in Kilometres

WARNING : Map not to be used for navigation purposes

See Map 4

North
Miladhunmadulu
Atoll

Fushifarurah

Fushi Faru

Noomara Kandu

Feydhoo
(1026)
(50m)

See Map 1

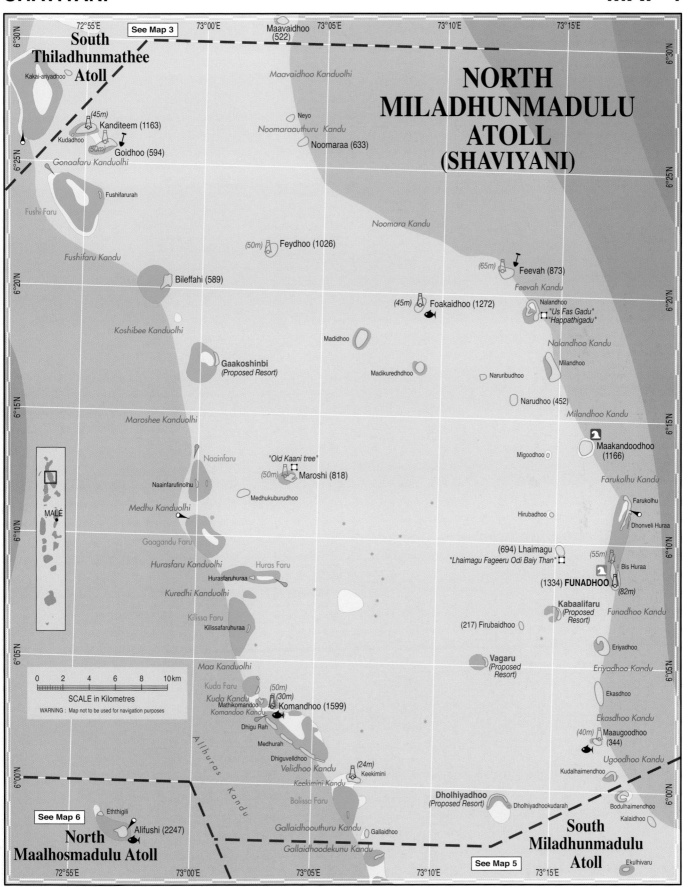

South
Thiladhunmathee
Atoll

See Map 3

Maavaidhoo
(522)

Kakai-ariyadhoo

Maavaidhoo Kanduolhi

NORTH
MILADHUNMADULU
ATOLL
(SHAVIYANI)

Neyo

(45m)

Kanditeem (1163)

Noomaraauthuru Kandu

Kudadhoo

(50m)

Goidhoo (594)

Noomaraa (633)

Gonaafaru Kanduolhi

Fushifarurah

Fushi Faru

Noomara Kandu

Fushifaru Kandu

(50m)

Feydhoo (1026)

(65m)

Feevah (873)

Feevah Kandu

Bileffahi (589)

(45m)

Foakaidhoo (1272)

Nalandhoo
"Us Fas Gadu"
"Happathigadu"

Koshibee Kanduolhi

Madidhoo

Nalandhoo Kandu

Milandhoo

Gaakoshinbi
(Proposed Resort)

Madikuredhdhoo

Naruribudhoo

Maroshee Kanduolhi

Narudhoo (452)

Milandhoo Kandu

Naainfaru

"Old Kaani tree"

Migoodhoo

Maakandoodhoo
(1166)

Naainfarufinolhu

(50m)

Maroshi (818)

Farukolhu Kandu

Medhu Kanduolhi

Medhukuburudhoo

Hirubadhoo

Farukolhu

Dhonveli Huraa

Gaagandu Faru

(694) Lhaimagu
"Lhaimagu Fageeru Odi Baiy Than"

(55m)

Bis Huraa

Hurasfaru Kanduolhi

Huras Faru

(1334) FUNADHOO

(82m)

Hurastaruhuraa

Kuredhi Kanduolhi

Kabaalifaru
(Proposed
Resort)

Funadhoo Kandu

Kilissa Faru

Kilissafaruhuraa

(217) Firubaidhoo

Eriyadhoo

MALÉ

Vagaru
(Proposed
Resort)

Eriyadhoo Kandu

Maa Kanduolhi

Ekasdhoo

0   2   4   6   8   10km

SCALE in Kilometres

WARNING : Map not to be used for navigation purposes

Kuda Faru

Kuda Kandu

(50m)

(30m)

Mathikomandoo

Komandoo Kandu

Komandhoo (1599)

Ekasdhoo Kandu

(40m)

Maaugoodhoo
(344)

Dhigu Rah

Medhurah

Ugoodhoo Kandu

Dhiguvelldhoo

Velidhoo Kandu

(24m)

Keekimini

Kudalhaimendhoo

Keekimini Kandu

Bolissa Faru

Dholhiyadhoo
(Proposed Resort)

Dholhiyadhookudarah

Bodulhaimendhoo

Kalaidhoo

See Map 6

Eththigili

North
Maalhosmadulu Atoll

Alifushi (2247)

Gallaidhoouthuru Kandu

Gallaidhoo

South
Miladhunmadulu
Atoll

Gallaidhoodekunu Kandu

See Map 5

Ekulhivaru

MAP 5

NOONU

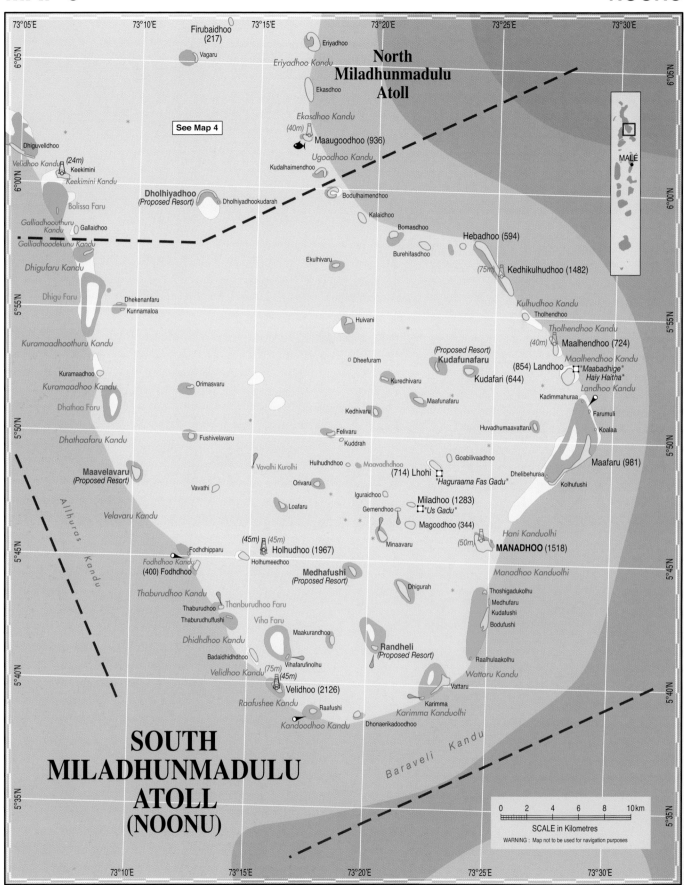

73°05'E 73°10'E 73°15'E 73°20'E 73°25'E 73°30'E

Firubaidhoo (217)

Eriyadhoo

North Miladhunmadulu Atoll

Vagaru

Eriyadhoo Kandu

Ekasdhoo

6°05'N

Ekasdhoo Kandu
(40m)

See Map 4

Maaugoodhoo (936)

Ugoodhoo Kandu

Kudalhaimendhoo

Dhiguvelidhoo

6°00'N

Velidhoo Kandu *(24m)*

Keekimini

Keekimini Kandu

Bodulhaimendhoo

Dholhiyadhoo *(Proposed Resort)* Dholhiyadhookudarah

Kalaidhoo

Bolissa Faru

Bomasdhoo

Galliadhoouthuru Kandu Gallaidhoo

Hebadhoo (594)

Burehifasdhoo

Galliadhoodekunu Kandu

Ekulhivaru

(75m) Kedhikulhudhoo (1482)

Dhigufaru Kandu

Kulhudhoo Kandu

Tholhendhoo

5°55'N

Dhigu Faru

Dhekenanfaru

Huivani

Tholhendhoo Kandu

Kunnamaloa

(40m) Maalhendhoo (724)

Kuramaadhoothuru Kandu

Dheefuram

(Proposed Resort) **Kudafunafaru**

Maalhendhoo Kandu

(854) Landhoo ☐*"Maabadhige" Haiy Haitha"*

Kuramaadhoo

Orimasvaru

Kuredhivaru

Kudafari (644)

Kadimmahuraa

Kuramaadhoo Kandu

Maafunafaru

5°50'N

Dhathaa Faru

Kedhivaru

Farumuli

Huvadhumaavattaru

Koalaa

Fushivelavaru

Felivaru

Kuddrah

Dhathaafaru Kandu

Maavelavaru *(Proposed Resort)*

Vavalhi Kurolhi

Hulhudhdhoo *Maavadhdhoo*

Goabilivaadhoo

Dhelibehuraa

Maafaru (981)

(714) Lhohi ☐

Kolhufushi

Vavathi

Orivaru

"Haguraama Fas Gadu"

Velavaru Kandu

Iguraidhoo

Loafaru

Gemendhoo

Miladhoo (1283) ☐*"Us Gadu"*

5°45'N

Allhuraas Kandu

(45m) *(45m)*

Fodhdhipparu

Holhudhoo (1967)

Minaavaru

Magoodhoo (344)

Hani Kanduolhi

(50m) **MANADHOO (1518)**

Holhumeedhoo

(400) Fodhdhoo

Fodhdhoo Kandu

Manadhoo Kanduolhi

Thaburudhoo Kandu

Medhafushi *(Proposed Resort)*

Dhigurah

Thoshigadukolhu

Thaburudhoo *Thanburudhoo Faru*

Medhufaru

Thaburudhuffushi

Kudafushi

Viha Faru

Bodufushi

5°40'N

Dhidhdhoo Kandu

Maakurandhoo

Randheli *(Proposed Resort)*

Badaidhidhdhoo

Vihafarufinolhu

Raalhulaakolhu

Velidhoo Kandu *(75m)*

(45m)

Vattaru

Velidhoo (2126)

Karimma

Wattaru Kandu

Raafushee Kandu Raafushi

Karimma Kanduolhi

Kandoodhoo Kandu Dhonaerikadoodhoo

Baraveli Kandu

SOUTH MILADHUNMADULU ATOLL (NOONU)

5°35'N

MALÉ

0 2 4 6 8 10km

SCALE in Kilometres

WARNING : Map not to be used for navigation purposes

73°10'E 73°15'E 73°20'E 73°25'E 73°30'E

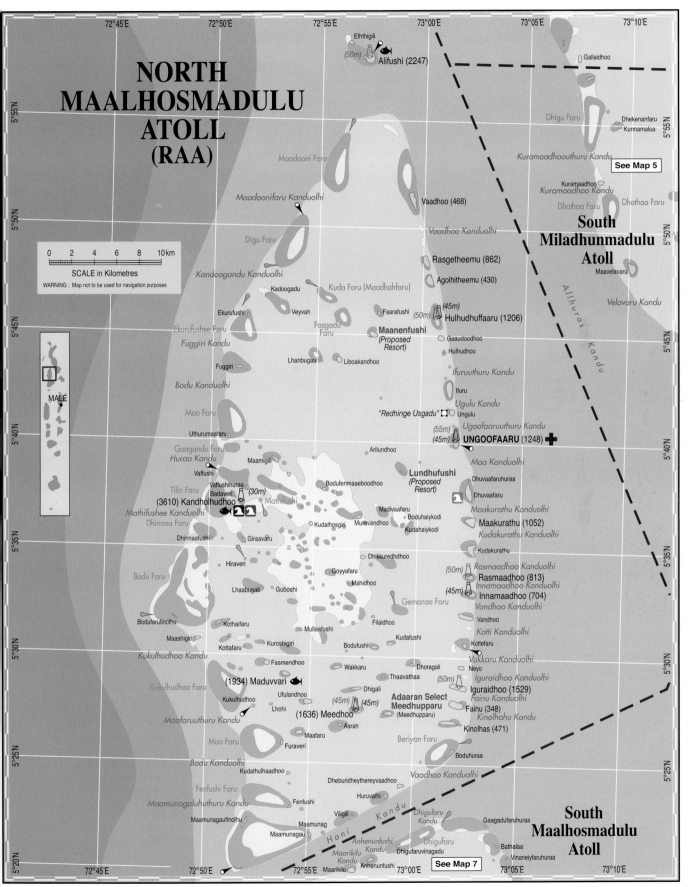

NORTH MAALHOSMADULU ATOLL (RAA)

SCALE in Kilometres
0 2 4 6 8 10km
WARNING : Map not to be used for navigation purposes

MALÉ

Eththigili
(50m) Alifushi (2247)
Gallaidhoo
Dhigu Faru
Dhekenanfaru
Kunnamaloa
Maadooni Faru
See Map 5
Kuramaadhoouthuru Kandu
Maadoonifaru Kanduolhi
Kuramaadhoo
Kuramaadhoo Kandu
Vaadhoo (468)
Dhathaa Faru
Dhathaa Faru
South Miladhunmadulu Atoll
Digu Faru
Vaadhoo Kanduolhi
Rasgetheemu (862)
Maavelavaru
Kandoogandu Kanduolhi
Kadoogadu
Agolhitheemu (430)
Velavaru Kandu
Kuda Faru (Maadhahfaru)
Ekurufushi
Veyvah
Faarafushi
(50m) *(45m)* Hulhudhuffaaru (1206)
Ekurufushee Faru
Fasgadu Faru
Maanenfushi
(Proposed Resort)
Gaaudoodhoo
Fuggiri Kandu
Lhanbugau
Liboakandhoo
Hulhudhoo
Fuggiri
Ifuruuthuru Kandu
Bodu Kanduolhi
Ifuru
Ugulu Kandu
Maa Faru
"Redhinge Usgadu"
Ungulu
Ugoofaaruuthuru Kandu
Uthurumaafaru
(55m) *(45m)* **UNGOOFAARU** (1248) ✚
Gaagandu Faru
Arilundhoo
Huraa Kandu
Maamigili
Maa Kanduolhi
Vaffushi
Dhuvaafaruhuraa
Vaffushihuraa
Badaveri *(30m)*
Lundhufushi
(Proposed Resort)
Dhuvaafaru
Tilin Faru
(3610) Kandholhudhoo
Mathifushi
Maakurathu Kanduolhi
Mathifushee Kanduolhi
Boduferimaaeboodhoo
Dhinnaa Faru
Dhinnaafushi
Giraavaru
Madivaafaru
Maakurathu (1052)
Kudalhosgiri
Muravandhoo
Boduhaiykodi
Kudakurathu Kanduolhi
Hiraveri
Kudahaiykodi
Kudakurathu
Dhikkuredhdhoo
(50m) Rasmaadhoo Kanduolhi
Bodu Faru
Goyyafaru
Rasmaadhoo (813)
Innamaadhoo Kanduolhi
Lhaabugali
Guboshi
Mahidhoo
(45m) **Innamaadhoo** (704)
Vandhoo Kanduolhi
Gemanaa Faru
Vandhoo
BodufaruTinolhu
Filaidhoo
Kotti Kanduolhi
Maashigiri
Kothaifaru
Mullaafushi
Kudafushi
Kottefaru
Kottafaru
Kuroshigiri
Bodufushi
Vakkaru Kanduolhi
Kukulhudhoo Kandu
Fasmendhoo
Wakkaru
Dhoragali
Neyo
Iguraidhoo Kanduolhi
Kukulhudhoo Faru
Thaavathaa
(50m) **Iguraidhoo** (1529)
(1934) Maduvvari
Ufulandhoo
Dhigali
Fainu Kanduolhi
Kukulhudhoo
(45m) *(45m)* **Fainu** (348)
Lhohi
Adaaran Select Meedhupparu
(Meedhupparu)
Kinolhohu Kandu
Maafaruuthuru Kandu
(1636) Meedhoo
Aarah
Kinolhas (471)
Maafaru
Maa Faru
Furaveri
Beriyan Faru
Bodu Kanduolhi
Boduhuraa
Kudathulhaadhoo
Dheburidheythereyvaadhoo
Vaadhoo Kanduolhi
Fenfushi Faru
Huruvalhi
Maamunagaluhuthuru Kandu
Fenfushi
Gaagadufaruhuraa
South Maalhosmadulu Atoll
Viligili
Maamunag
Dhigufaru Kandu
Maamunagaufinolhu
Maamunagau
Hani Kandu
Anhenunfushi
Dhigufaru
Bathalaa
Maarikilu Kandu
Dhigufaruvinagadu
Vinaneiyfaruhuraa
Maarikilu Anhenunfushi
See Map 7

MAP 7

BAA

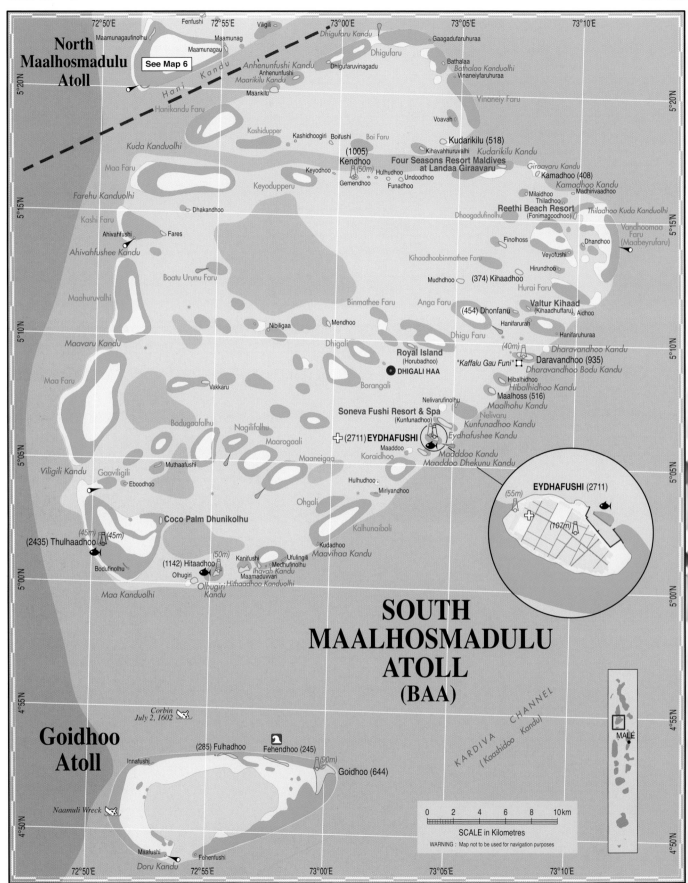

North Maalhosmadulu Atoll

See Map 6

72°50'E
Fenfushi
72°55'E
Viligili
73°00'E
Dhigufaru Kandu
Gaagadufaruhuraa
73°05'E
73°10'E

Maamunagaufinolhu
Maamunag
Maamunagau
Dhigufaru
Bathalaa *Kanduolhi*
Vinaneiyfaruhuraa

Anhenunfushi Kandu
Anhenunfushi
Dhigufaruvinagadu

Maarikilu Kandu
Maarikilu
Voavah
Vinaneiy Faru

Hani Kandu

Hanikandu Faru

Kuda Kanduolhi
Kashidupper
Kashidhoogiri Boifushi
Boi Faru
Kudarikilu (518)
Kihavahhuruvalhi
Kudarikilu Kandu

(1005)
Kendhoo
(50m)
Four Seasons Resort Maldives
at Landaa Giraavaru
Giraavaru Kandu
Kamadhoo (408)

Maa Faru
Keyodhoo
Hulhudhoo
Undoodhoo
Funadhoo
Kamadhoo Kandu
Milaidhoo
Madhirivaadhoo

Keyodupperu
Gemendhoo
Thiladhoo

Farehu Kanduolhi
Dhakandhoo
Reethi Beach Resort
(Fonimagoodhoo)
Dhoogadufinolhu
Thiladhoo Kuda Kanduolhi

Kashi Faru
Ahivahfushi
Fares
Finolhoss
Dhandhoo
Vandhoomaa Faru
(Maabeyrufaru)

Ahivahfushee Kandu
Veyofushi

Boatu Urunu Faru
Kihaadhoobinmathee Fan
Hirundhoo
Hurai Faru

Maahuruvalhi
Mudhdhoo
(374) Kihaadhoo
Valtur Kihaad
(Kihaadhuffaru) Aidhoo

Binmathee Faru
Anga Faru
(454) Dhonfanu
Hanifarurah
Hanifaruhuraa

Maavaru Kandu
Nibiligaa
Mendhoo
Dhigu Faru
(40m)
Dharavandhoo Kandu

Dhigali
"Kaffalu Gau Funi"
Daravandhoo (935)
Dharavandhoo Bodu Kandu

Maa Faru
Vakkaru
Royal Island
(Horubadhoo)
● DHIGALI HAA
Hibalhidhoo
Hibalhidhoo Kandu
Maalhoss (516)

Borangali
Nelivarufinolhu
Maalhohu Kandu
Nelivaru

Bodugaafalhu
Nagilifalhu
Soneva Fushi Resort & Spa
(Kunfunadhoo)
Kunfunadhoo Kandu

Maarogaali
✚ (2711) EYDHAFUSHI
Eydhafushee Kandu
Maaddoo

Muthaafushi
Maaneigaa
Koraidhoo
Maaddoo Kandu
Maaddoo Dhekunu Kandu

Viligili Kandu
Gaaviligili
Eboodhoo
Hulhudhoo
Miriyandhoo

Ohgali
(55m)
EYDHAFUSHI (2711)

Coco Palm Dhunikolhu
Kalhunaiboli
(107m)

(45m)   (45m)
(2435) Thulhaadhoo
Bodufinolhu
(1142) Hitaadhoo
(50m)
Kanifushi Ufulingili
Medhufinolhu
Ihavah Kandu
Maamaduvvari
Kudadhoo
Maavihaa Kandu

Olhugiri
*Olhugiri
Kandu*
Hithaadhoo Kanduolhi

Maa Kanduolhi

SOUTH
MAALHOSMADULU
ATOLL
(BAA)

Corbin
July 2, 1602

Goidhoo Atoll
(285) Fulhadhoo
Fehendhoo (245)
(90m)
Goidhoo (644)
Innafushi

Naamuli Wreck

KARDIVA CHANNEL
(Kaashidoo Kandu)

MALÉ

0   2   4   6   8   10km
SCALE in Kilometres
WARNING : Map not to be used for navigation purposes

Maafushi
Doru Kandu
Fehenfushi

72°50'E
72°55'E
73°00'E
73°05'E
73°10'E

5°20'N
5°15'N
5°10'N
5°05'N
5°00'N
4°55'N
4°50'N

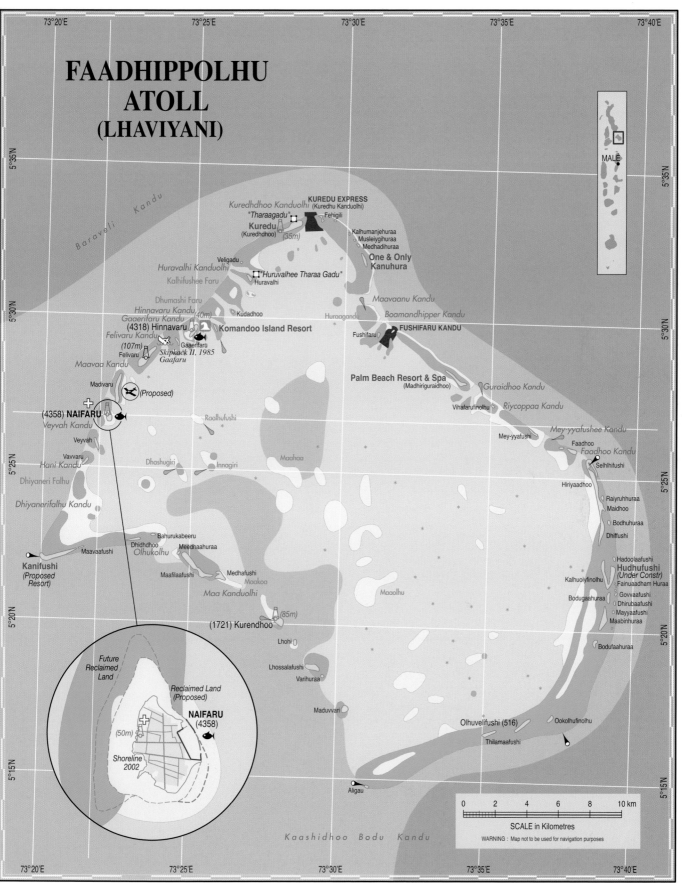

FAADHIPPOLHU
ATOLL
(LHAVIYANI)

73°20'E　　73°25'E　　73°30'E　　73°35'E　　73°40'E

5°35'N

MALE

Baraveli Kandu

KUREDU EXPRESS
(Kuredhu Kanduolhi)

Kuredhdhoo Kanduolhi
"Tharaagadu"
Kuredu
(Kuredhdhoo)
Fehigili
(35m)

Kalhumanjehuraa
Musleiygihuraa
Medhadihuraa

**One & Only
Kanuhura**

Veligadu
Huravalhi Kanduolhi
Kalhifushee Faru
□ "Huruvalhee Tharaa Gadu"
Huravalhi

Maavaanu Kandu

Dhumashi Faru
Hinnavaru Kandu (40m)
Gaaerifaru Kandu
Kudadhoo
Huraagandu
Boamandhipper Kandu

(4318) Hinnavaru
Komandoo Island Resort

5°30'N

Fushifaru
FUSHIFARU KANDU

Felivaru Kandu
(107m)
Felivaru
Gaaerifaru
Skipjack II, 1985
Gaafaru

Maavaa Kandu

Palm Beach Resort & Spa
(Madhiriguraidhoo)

Vihafarufinolhu
Guraidhoo Kandu
Riycoppaa Kandu

Madivaru
✈ (Proposed)

(4358) **NAIFARU** ✚
Veyvah Kandu
🐟

Raalhufushi

Mey-yyafushi
Mey-yyafushee Kandu

Faadhoo
Faadhoo Kandu
Selhlhifushi

Veyvah
Vavvaru
Hani Kandu

5°25'N

Dhashugiri
Innagiri

Maahaa

Hiriyaadhoo

Raiyruhhuraa
Maidhoo
Bodhuhuraa
Dhiffushi

Dhiyaneri Falhu

Dhiyanerifalhu Kandu

Bahurukabeeru
Dhidhdhoo
Olhukolhu
Meedhaahuraa

Maavaafushi

Maafilaafushi
Medhafushi
Moakoa

Maa Kanduolhi

Maaolhu

Hadoolaafushi
Hudhufushi
(Under Constr)
Fainuaadham Huraa
Kalhuoiyfinolhu
Govvaafushi
Bodugaahuraa
Dhirubaafushi
Mayyaafushi
Maabinhuraa

5°20'N

(85m)

(1721) Kurendhoo

Lhohi
Bodufaahuraa

Lhossalafushi
Varihuraa

Maduvvari

Olhuvelifushi (516)
Ookolhufinolhu
Thilamaafushi

Aligau

Kaashidhoo Bodu Kandu

Naifaru inset
Future
Reclaimed
Land

Reclaimed Land
(Proposed)

NAIFARU
✚
(4358)
🐟
(50m)

Shoreline
2002

SCALE in Kilometres

| 0 | 2 | 4 | 6 | 8 | 10 km |

WARNING : Map not to be used for navigation purposes

73°20'E　　73°25'E　　73°30'E　　73°35'E　　73°40'E

33

MAP 9

KAAFU

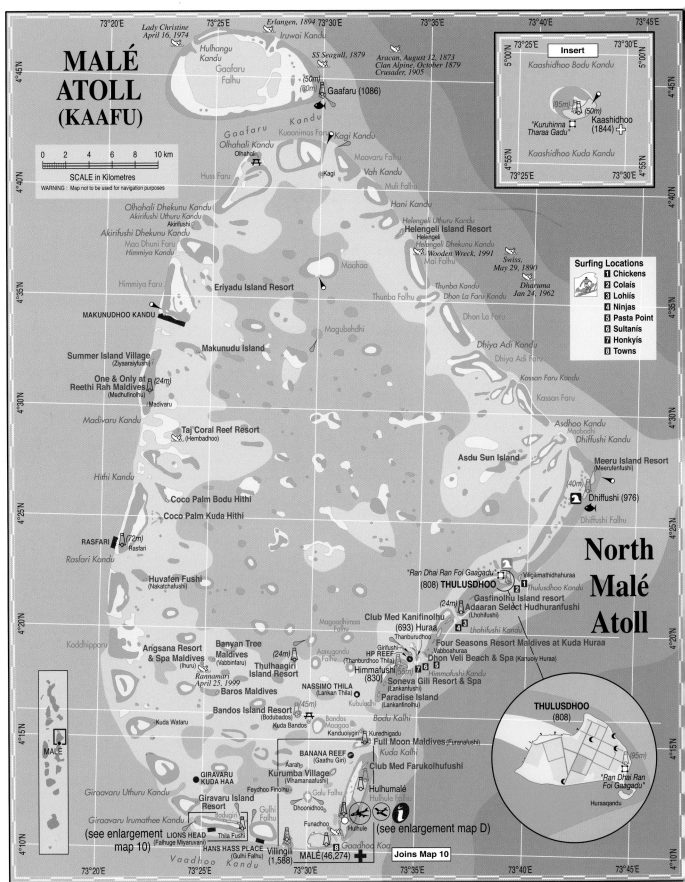

MALÉ ATOLL (KAAFU)

SCALE in Kilometres
0 2 4 6 8 10 km
WARNING : Map not to be used for navigation purposes

Insert
73°25'E 73°30'E
5°00'N
Kaashidhoo Bodu Kandu
(85m) *(50m)*
"Kuruhinna Tharaa Gadu" Kaashidhoo (1844)
4°55'N
Kaashidhoo Kuda Kandu
73°25'E 73°30'E

Lady Christine April 16, 1974
Erlangen, 1894
Hulhangu Kandu
Iruwai Kandu
SS Seagull, 1879
Gaafaru Falhu
Aracan, August 12, 1873
Clan Alpine, October 1879
Crusader, 1905
(50m)
(80m) Gaafaru (1086)
Gaafaru Olhahali Kandu
Kandu
Gaafaru
Kuoonimas Faru
Olhahali Kagi Kandu
Huss Faru Kagi
Maavaru Falhu
Vah Kandu
Muli Falhu

Olhahali Dhekunu Kandu
Akirifushi Uthuru Kandu Akirifushi
Akirifushi Dhekunu Kandu
Maa Dhuni Faru
Himmiya Kandu
Hani Kandu
Helengeli Uthuru Kandu
Helengeli Island Resort
Helengeli
Helengeli Dhekunu Kandu
Mai Falhu *Wooden Wreck, 1991*
Swiss, May 29, 1890
Himmiya Faru
Maahaa
Eriyadu Island Resort
Thunba Kandu *Dharuma Jan 24, 1962*
Thunba Falhu *Dhon La Faru Kandu*
Magubehdhi
Dhon La Faru
MAKUNUDHOO KANDU
Dhiya Adi Kandu
Makunudu Island *Dhiya Adi Faru*
Kassan Faru Kandu
Summer Island Village
(Ziyaaraiyfushi)
Kassan Faru
One & Only at Reethi Rah Maldives
(Medhufinolhu) *(24m)*
Madivaru
Madivaru Kandu
Taj Coral Reef Resort
(Hembadhoo)
Asdhoo Kandu
Maabadhi
Dhiffushi Kandu
Asdu Sun Island
Meeru Island Resort
(Meerufenfushi)
Hithi Kandu
(40m)
Coco Palm Bodu Hithi
Dhiffushi (976)
Coco Palm Kuda Hithi
Dhiffushi Falhu
RASFARI *(72m)*
Rasfari
Rasfari Kandu

North Malé Atoll

Surfing Locations
1 Chickens
2 Colaís
3 Lohiís
4 Ninjas
5 Pasta Point
6 Sultanís
7 Honkyís
8 Towns

Huvafen Fushi
(Nakatchafushi)
"Ran Dhai Ran Foi Gaagadu" *Viligilimathidhahuraa*
(808) **THULUSDHOO**
Thulusdhoo Kandu
Gasfinolhu Island resort
(24m) **Adaaran Select Hudhuranfushi**
(Lhohifushi)
Club Med Kanifinolhu
(693) **Huraa** *Lhohifushi Kandu*
Thanburudhoo
Four Seasons Resort Maldives at Kuda Huraa
Koddhipparu
Magaadhimaa Falhu
Vabboahuraa
Girifushi **Dhon Veli Beach & Spa** *(Kanuoiy Huraa)*
Angsana Resort & Spa Maldives
(Ihuru)
Banyan Tree Maldives
(Vabbinfaru) *(24m)*
HP REEF
(Thanburdhoo Thila)
Aanugandu Falhu
Himmafushi *(55m)*
(830)
Thulhaagiri Island Resort
Rannamari April 25, 1999
Himmafushi Kandu
Soneva Gili Resort & Spa
(Lankanfushi)
Baros Maldives
NASSIMO THILA
(Lankan Thila)
Paradise Island
(Lankanfinolhu)
Bandos Island Resort
(Bodubados) *(45m)*
Kubuladhi
Full Moon Maldives *(Furanafushi)*
Kuda Bandos
Bodu Kalhi
Kuda Wataru
Bandos Maagaa
Kanduoiygiri Kuredhigadu
Kuda Kalhi
BANANA REEF *(Gaathu Giri)*
Club Med Farukolhufushi
MALÉ
Aarah
GIRAVARU KUDA HAA
Kurumba Village
(Vihamanaafushi)
Giraavaru Uthuru Kandu
Feydhoo Finolhu
Galu Falhu
Hulhumalé
Giravaru Island Resort
Bodugiri *Hulhule Falhu*
Giraavaru Irumathee Kandu
Thila Fushi
Dhoonidhoo
Gulhi Falhu
Funadhoo Hulhule
(see enlargement map 10) **LIONS HEAD**
(Falhuge Miyaruvani)
HANS HASS PLACE
(Gulhi Falhu) **Villingili** (1,588)
MALÉ (46,274)
(see enlargement map D)
Vaadhoo Kandu
Joins Map 10

THULUSDHOO (808)
(95m)
"Ran Dhai Ran Foi Gaagadu"
Huraaqandu

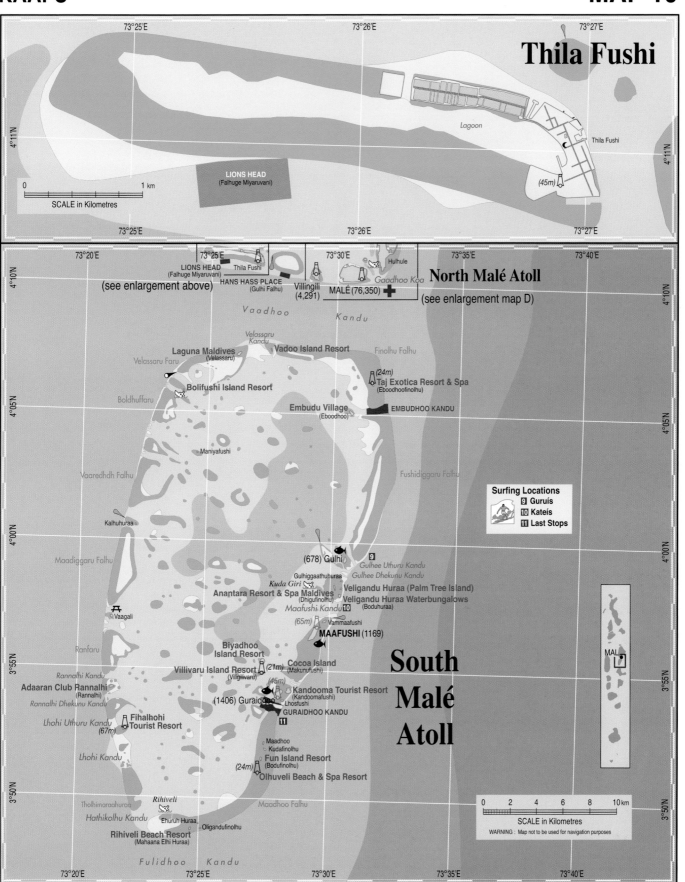

Thila Fushi

4°11'N

Lagoon

Thila Fushi

LIONS HEAD
(Falhuge Miyaruvani)

(45m)

0   1 km
SCALE in Kilometres

73°25'E   73°26'E   73°27'E

73°20'E   73°25'E   73°30'E   73°35'E   73°40'E

4°10'N

LIONS HEAD
(Falhuge Miyaruvani)   Thila Fushi   Hulhule

(see enlargement above)   HANS HASS PLACE
(Gulhi Falhu)   Villingili
(4,291)   MALÉ (76,350) ✚   *Gaadhoo Koa*   **North Malé Atoll**

(see enlargement map D)

Vaadhoo   Kandu

*Velassaru
Kandu*

Laguna Maldives
(Velassaru)   **Vadoo Island Resort**   Finolhu Falhu

Velassaru Faru

Bolifushi Island Resort   *(24m)* Taj Exotica Resort & Spa
(Eboodhoofinolhu)

Boldhuffaru

Embudu Village   EMBUDHOO KANDU
(Eboodhoo)

Maniyafushi

Vaaredhdh Falhu   *Fushidiggaru Falhu*

4°05'N

Surfing Locations
9 Guruís
10 Kateís
11 Last Stops

Kalhuhuraa

Maadiggaru Falhu

4°00'N

(678) Gulhi
Gulhee Uthuru Kandu
Gulhiggaathuhuraa   *Gulhee Dhekunu Kandu*
Kuda Giri   **Veligandu Huraa (Palm Tree Island)**
Anantara Resort & Spa Maldives   **Veligandu Huraa Waterbungalows**
(Dhigufinolhu)   (Boduhuraa)
Maafushi Kandu 10
(65m)   Vammaafushi
Vaagali   **MAAFUSHI** (1169)

Ranfaru

**Biyadhoo
Island Resort**

3°55'N

Rannalhi Kandu   **Villivaru Island Resort**   *(21m)*   **Cocoa Island**
(Vilighivaru)   (Makunufushi)   **South**
Adaaran Club Rannalhi   *(45m)*
(Rannalhi)
Rannalhi Dhekunu Kandu   (1406) Guraidhoo   **Kandooma Tourist Resort**   **Malé**
Lhosfushi   (Kandoomafushi)
Lhohi Uthuru Kandu   **Fihalhohi**   GURAIDHOO KANDU   **Atoll**
Tourist Resort
(67m)   11

Lhohi Kandu   Maadhoo
Kudafinolhu
Fun Island Resort
(Bodufinolhu)
(24m)   **Olhuveli Beach & Spa Resort**

3°50'N

Rihiveli
Tholhimaraahuraa   *Maadhoo Falhu*
Hathikolhu Kandu   Ehuruh Huraa
Oligandufinolhu
Rihiveli Beach Resort
(Mahaana Elhi Huraa)

Fulidhoo   Kandu

MALÉ

0   2   4   6   8   10km
SCALE in Kilometres
WARNING : Map not to be used for navigation purposes

73°20'E   73°25'E   73°30'E   73°35'E   73°40'E

Protected Marine Areas

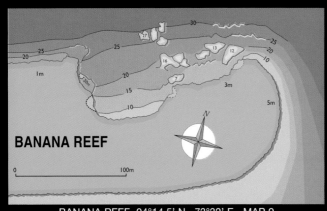

BANANA REEF   04°14.5' N   73°32' E   MAP 9

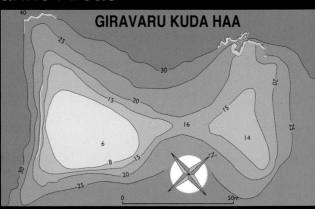

GIRAVARU KUDA HAA   04°12' N   73°24.5' E   MAP 9

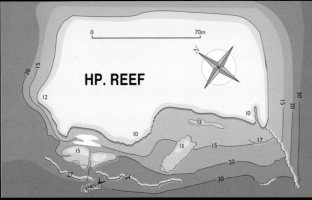

HP REEF   04°19' N   73°34.5' E   MAP 9

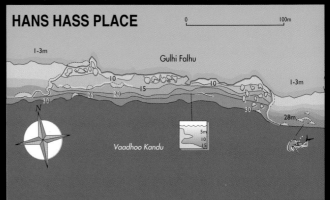

HANS HASS PLACE   04°10.5' N   73°28' E   MAP 9

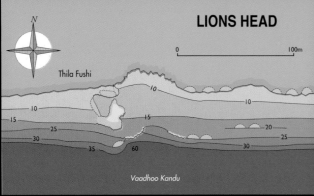

LIONS HEAD   04°11' N   73°25.5' E   MAP 9

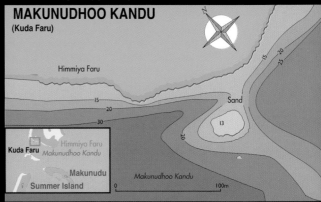

MAKUNUDHOO KANDU   04°34' N   73°23' E   MAP 9

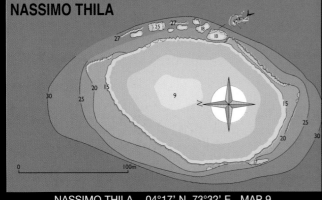

NASSIMO THILA   04°17' N   73°32' E   MAP 9

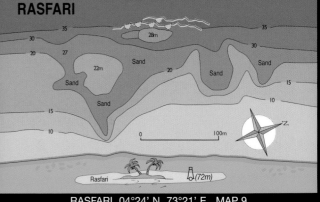

RASFARI   04°24' N   73°21' E   MAP 9

Protected Marine Areas

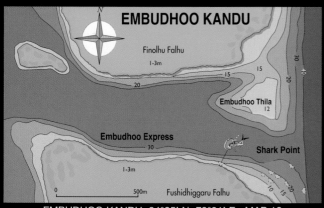

EMBUDHOO KANDU 04°05' N 73°31' E MAP 10

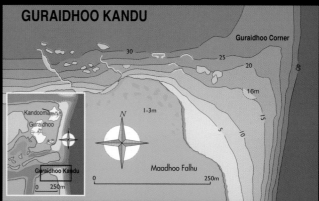

GURAIDHOO KANDU 03°53.5' N 73°27' E MAP 10

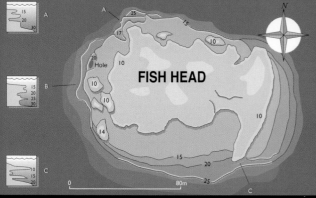

FISH HEAD 03°56' N 72°55' E MAP 11

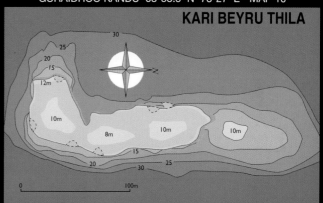

KARIBEYRU THILA 04°06' N 72°57' E MAP 11

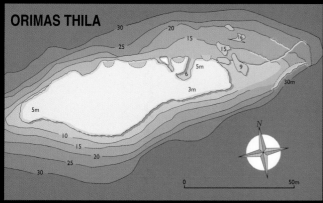

ORIMAS THILA 03°59' N 72°57' E MAP 11

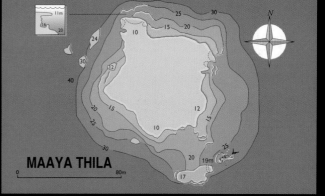

MAAYA THILA 04°05' N 72°51.5' E MAP 11

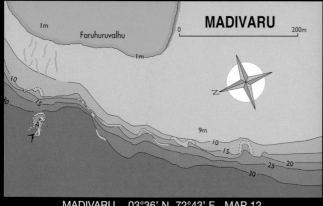

MADIVARU 03°36' N 72°43' E MAP 12

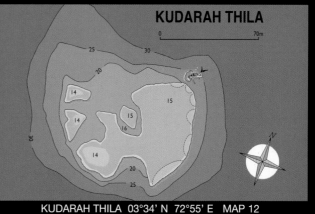

KUDARAH THILA 03°34' N 72°55' E MAP 12

Protected Marine Areas

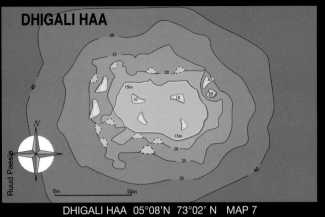

DHIGALI HAA 05°08'N 73°02' N MAP 7

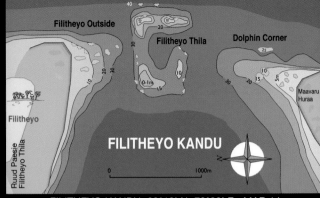

FILITHEYO KANDU 03°13' N 73°02' E MAP 14

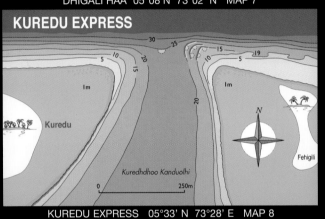

KUREDU EXPRESS 05°33' N 73°28' E MAP 8

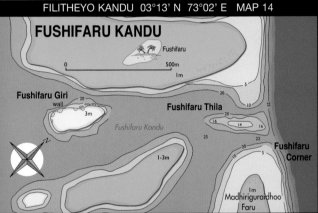

FUSHIFARU KANDU 05°29' N 73°31' E MAP 8

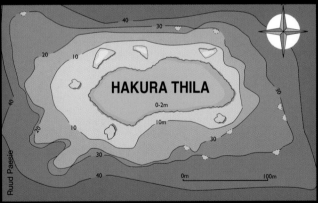

HAKURA THILA 02°57' N 73°33' E MAP 16

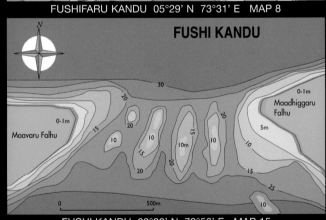

FUSHI KANDU 03°00' N 72°56' E MAP 15

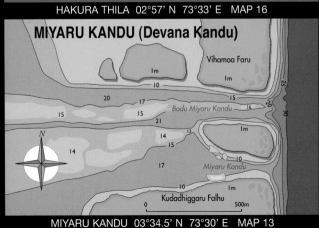

MIYARU KANDU 03°34.5' N 73°30' E MAP 13

VATTARU KANDU 03°13' N 73°26' E MAP 13

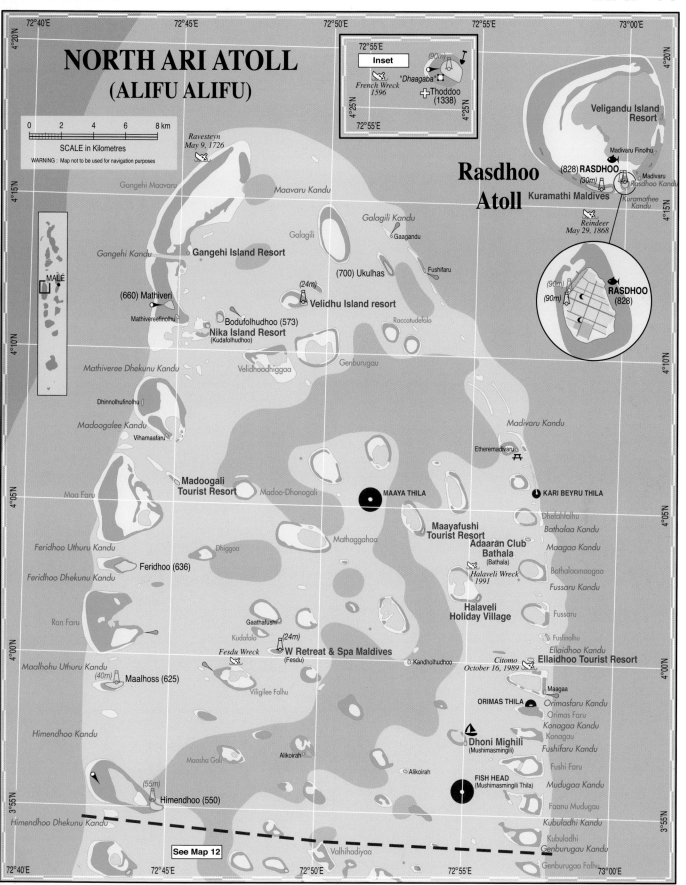

MAP 12

ALIFU DHAALU

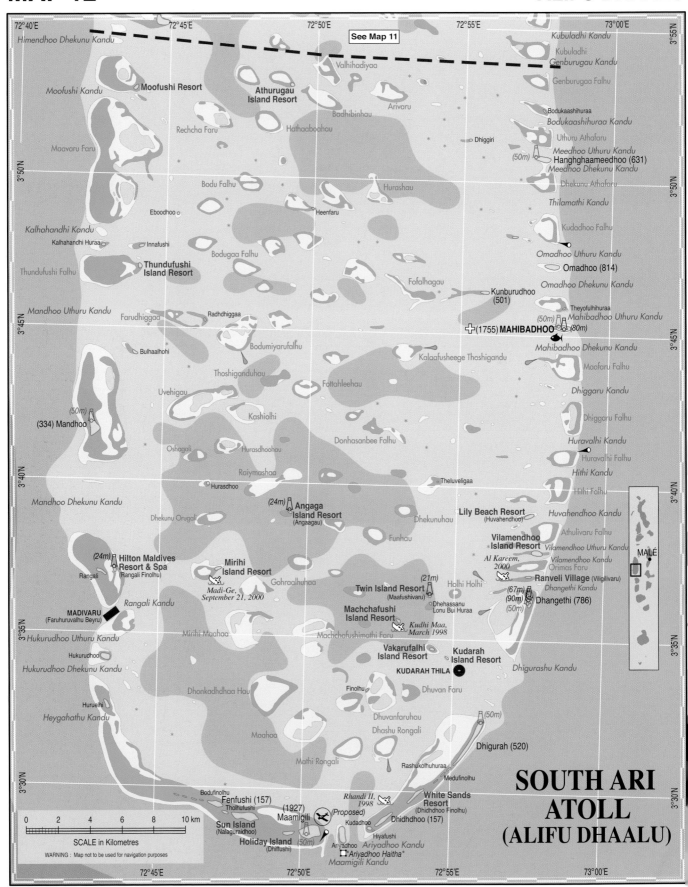

72°40'E · 72°45'E · 72°50'E · 72°55'E · 73°00'E

Himendhoo Dhekunu Kandu

3°55'N

Kubuladhi Dhekunu Kandu

Kubuladhi
Genburugau Kandu

Moofushi Kandu
Moofushi Resort

Athurugau Island Resort

Valhihadiyaa

Genburugaa Falhu

Badhibinhau

Arivaru

Rechcha Faru

Hathaaboahau

Bodukaashihuraa
Bodukaashihuraa Kandu
Uthuru Athafaru

○ *Dhiggiri*

Meedhoo Uthuru Kandu

Maavaru Faru

3°50'N

(50m) **Hanghghaameedhoo (631)**
Meedhoo Dhekunu Kandu

Bodu Falhu

Hurashau

Thilamathi Kandu

○ *Eboodhoo*

Heenfaru

Dhekunu Athafaru

Kudadhoo Falhu

Kalhahandhi Kandu

Kalhahandhi Huraa

○ *Innafushi*

Bodugaa Falhu

Omadhoo Uthuru Kandu

Thundufushi Island Resort

Fofalhagau

Omadhoo (814)

Thundufushi Falhu

Farudhiggaa

Radhdhiggaa

Kunburudhoo (501)

Omadhoo Dhekunu Kandu

3°45'N

Mandhoo Uthuru Kandu

Theyofulhihuraa
(50m) *Mahibadhoo Uthuru Kandu*

✚ *(1755)* **MAHIBADHOO** *(80m)*

○ *Bulhaalhohi*

Bodumiyarufalhu

Mahibadhoo Dhekunu Kandu

(50m) **(334) Mandhoo**

Thoshiganduhau

Kalaafusheege Thoshigandu

Maafaru Falhu

Uvehigau

Fottahleehau

Dhiggaru Kandu

Kashiolhi

Dhiggaru Falhu

3°40'N

Donhasanbee Falhu

Huravalhi Kandu

Oshagali

Hurasdhoohau

Huravalhi Falhu

Raiymashaa

Hithi Kandu

○ *Theluveligaa*

Hithi Falhu

Hurasdhoo ○

Lily Beach Resort
(Huvahendhoo)

Huvahendhoo Kandu

(24m) **Angaga Island Resort**
(Angaagau)

Dhekunu Orugali

Dhekunuhau

Athulivaru Falhu

Funhau

Vilamendhoo Island Resort

Vilamendhoo Uthuru Kandu

MALÉ

3°35'N

(24m) **Hilton Maldives Resort & Spa**
(Rangali Finolhu)

Mirihi Island Resort

Al Kareem, 2000

Vilamendhoo Kandu
Orimas Faru

Rangali

Gohraalhuhau

Madi-Ge, September 21, 2000

(21m)
Twin Island Resort
(Maafushivaru)

Holhi Holhi

Ranveli Village *(Viligilivaru)*

Dhangethi Kandu

Rangali Kandu

MADIVARU
(Faruhuruvalhu Beyru)

Dhehassanu
Lonu Bui Huraa

(67m)

Dhangethi (786)

(90m)
(50m)

Machchafushi Island Resort

Kudhi Maa, March 1998

Hukurudhoo Uthuru Kandu

Mirihi-Maahaa

Machchafushimathi Faru

Vakarufalhi Island Resort

Kudarah Island Resort

Hukurudhoo ○

Dhigurashu Kandu

Hukurudhoo Dhekunu Kandu

KUDARAH THILA ●

Heygahathu Kandu

Huruelhi

Finolhu

Dhuvan Faru

Dhonkadhdhaa Hau

(50m)

Dhuvanfaruhau

Dhashu Rongali

Dhigurah (520)

3°30'N

Maahaa

Mathi Rongali

Rashukolhuhuraa

SOUTH ARI ATOLL (ALIFU DHAALU)

○ *Medufinolhu*

Bodufinolhu

Fenfushi (157)
Tholhufushi

(1927)

Rhandi II, 1998

White Sands Resort
(Dhidhdhoo Finolhu)

Dhidhdhoo (157)

Maamigili

(Proposed)

Sun Island
(Nalaguraidhoo)

Kudadhoo

Holiday Island *(50m)*
(Dhiffushi)

Ariyadhoo

Hiyafushi

Ariyadhoo Kandu

□ *"Ariyadhoo Haitha"*
Maamigili Kandu

72°45'E · 72°50'E · 72°55'E · 73°00'E

SCALE in Kilometres
0 2 4 6 8 10 km

WARNING : Map not to be used for navigation purposes

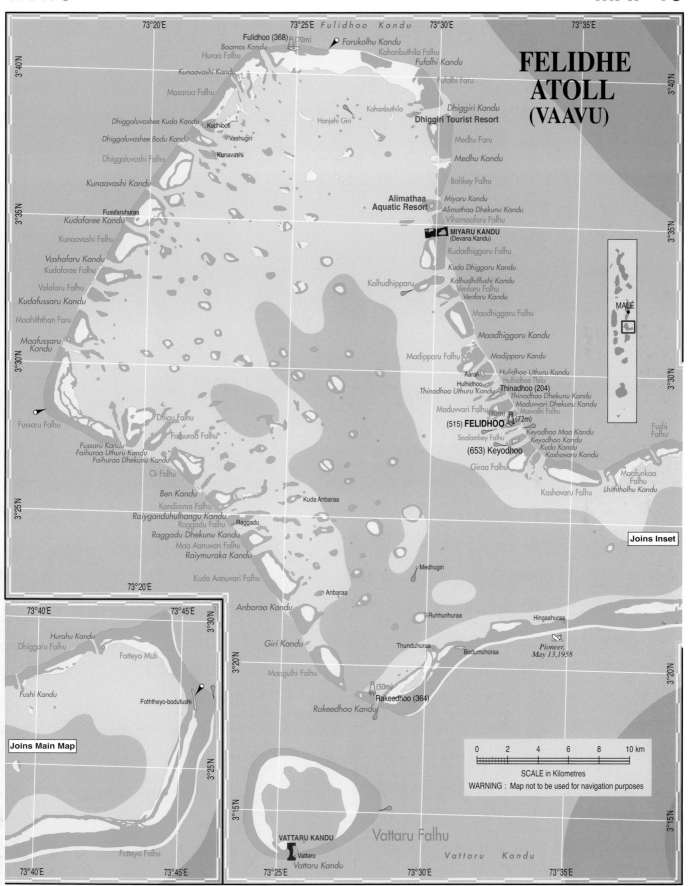

FELIDHE ATOLL (VAAVU)

73°20'E · 73°25'E · *Fulidhoo Kandu* · 73°30'E · 73°35'E

Fulidhoo (368) (70m)
Boamas Kandu
Huraa Falhu
Farukolhu Kandu
Kahanbuthila Falhu
Kunaavashi Kandu
Fufalhi Kandu
Masaraa Falhu
Futalhi Faru

Dhiggaluvashee Kuda Kandu · Kudhiboli
Kahanbuthila
Hanjehi Giri
Dhiggiri Kandu
Dhiggiri Tourist Resort
Dhiggaluvashee Bodu Kandu · Vashugiri
Medhu Faru
Kunavashi
Medhu Kandu
Dhiggaluvashi Falhu
Bolikey Falhu

Kunaavashi Kandu
Miyaru Kandu
Alimathaa Aquatic Resort
Alimathaa Dhekunu Kandu
Vihamaafaru Falhu
Fussfaruhuraa
MIYARU KANDU (Devana Kandu)
Kudafaree Kandu
Kudadhiggaru Falhu
Kunaavashi Falhu
Kuda Dhiggaru Kandu
Vashafaru Kandu
Kolhudhiffushi Kandu
Kudafaree Falhu
Kolhudhipparu
Venfaru Falhu
Valafaru Falhu
Venfaru Kandu
Kudafussaru Kandu
Maadhiggaru Falhu
Maahiththan Faru
Maadhiggaru Kandu
Maafussaru Kandu
Madipparu Falhu
Madipparu Kandu
Aarah
Hulidhoo Uthuru Kandu
Hulhidhoo · *Hulidhoo Thila*
Thinadhoo Uthuru Kandu · Thinadhoo (204)
Fussaru Falhu
Thinadhoo Dhekunu Kandu
Maduvvari Dhekunu Kandu
Maduvvari Falhu · *Masvalhi Falhu*
Dhigu Falhu
(80m) (72m)
Faiburaa Falhu
(515) **FELIDHOO**
Keyodhoo Maa Kandu
Fussaru Kandu
Saalambey Falhu
Keyodhoo Kandu
Faihuraa Uthuru Kandu
(653) Keyodhoo
Kuda Kandu
Faihuraa Dhekunu Kandu
Kashavaru Kandu
Oi Falhu
Giraa Falhu
Ben Kandu
Kashavaru Falhu
Maafunkoa Falhu
Kandimma Falhu
Lhiththolhu Kandu
Raiyganduhulhangu Kandu
Kuda Anbaraa
Raggadu Falhu · Raggadu
Raggadu Dhekunu Kandu
Maa Aanuvari Falhu
Raiymuraka Kandu
Kuda Aanuvari Kandu
Medhugiri
Anbaraa
Anbaraa Kandu
Ruhhurihuraa
Hingaahuraa
Giri Kandu
Thunduhuraa · Bodumohoraa
Pioneer, May 13,1958
Maagulhi Falhu
(50m)
Rakeedhoo (364)
Rakeedhoo Kandu

MALÉ

Joins Inset

Fushi Falhu

73°40'E · 73°45'E · 3°30'N

Hurahu Kandu
Dhiggaru Falhu
Fotteyo Muli
Fushi Kandu
Foththeyo-bodufushi

Joins Main Map

Fotteyo Falhu

73°40'E · 73°45'E · 3°25'N

VATTARU KANDU
Vattaru
Vattaru Kandu
Vattaru Falhu
Vattaru Kandu

73°25'E · 73°30'E · 73°35'E

0 2 4 6 8 10 km

SCALE in Kilometres

WARNING : Map not to be used for navigation purposes

MAP 14

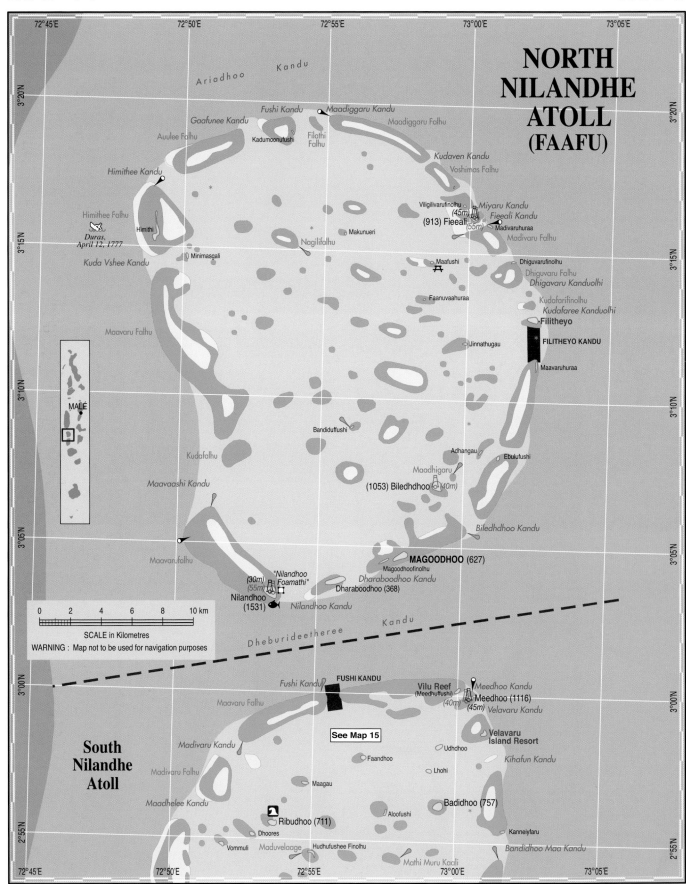

NORTH NILANDHE ATOLL (FAAFU)

Ariadhoo Kandu

3°20'N

Fushi Kandu   Maadiggaru Kandu

Gaafunee Kandu

Maadiggaru Falhu

Auulee Falhu   Kadumoonufushi   Filathi Falhu

Kudaven Kandu

Himithee Kandu   Voshimas Falhu

Viiligilivarufinolhu   Miyaru Kandu
(45m)   Fieeali Kandu

3°15'N   Himithee Falhu   (913) Fieeali   Madivaruhuraa

Duras, April 12, 1777   Himithi   (55m)   Madivaru Falhu

Makunueri   Dhiguvarufinolhu

Kuda Vshee Kandu   Minimasgali   Dhiguvaru Falhu
Maafushi   Dhigavaru Kanduolhi

Nagilifalhu   Kudafarifinolhu
Kudafaree Kanduolhi

Faanuvaahuraa   Filitheyo

Maavaru Falhu   FILITHEYO KANDU

Jinnathugau   Maavaruhuraa

3°10'N

MALÉ

Bandiduffushi   Adhangau   Ebulufushi

Kudafalhu

Maavaashi Kandu   Maadhigaru
(1053) Biledhdhoo   (40m)

Biledhdhoo Kandu

3°05'N

Maavarufalhu   MAGOODHOO (627)
Magoodhoofinolhu

"Nilandhoo   Dharaboodhoo Kandu
(30m) Foamathi"   Dharaboodhoo (368)
(55m)
Nilandhoo
(1531)   Nilandhoo Kandu

| 0 | 2 | 4 | 6 | 8 | 10 km |

SCALE in Kilometres

WARNING : Map not to be used for navigation purposes

Dheburideetheree   Kandu

3°00'N

Fushi Kandu   FUSHI KANDU   Vilu Reef   Meedhoo Kandu
(Meedhuffushi)   Meedhoo (1116)
Maavaru Falhu   (40m)   (45m)   Velavaru Kandu

See Map 15   Velavaru
Island Resort

South Nilandhe Atoll   Madivaru Kandu   Udhdhoo   Kihafun Kandu

Madivaru Falhu   Faandhoo   Lhohi

Maagau   Badidhoo (757)

Maadhelee Kandu   Aloofushi

Ribudhoo (711)   Kanneiyfaru

Dhoores

Vommuli   Maduvelaage   Hudhufushee Finolhu   Bandidhoo Maa Kandu

Mathi Muru Kaali

3°20'N
3°15'N
3°10'N
3°05'N
3°00'N
2°55'N

72°45'E   72°50'E   72°55'E   73°00'E   73°05'E

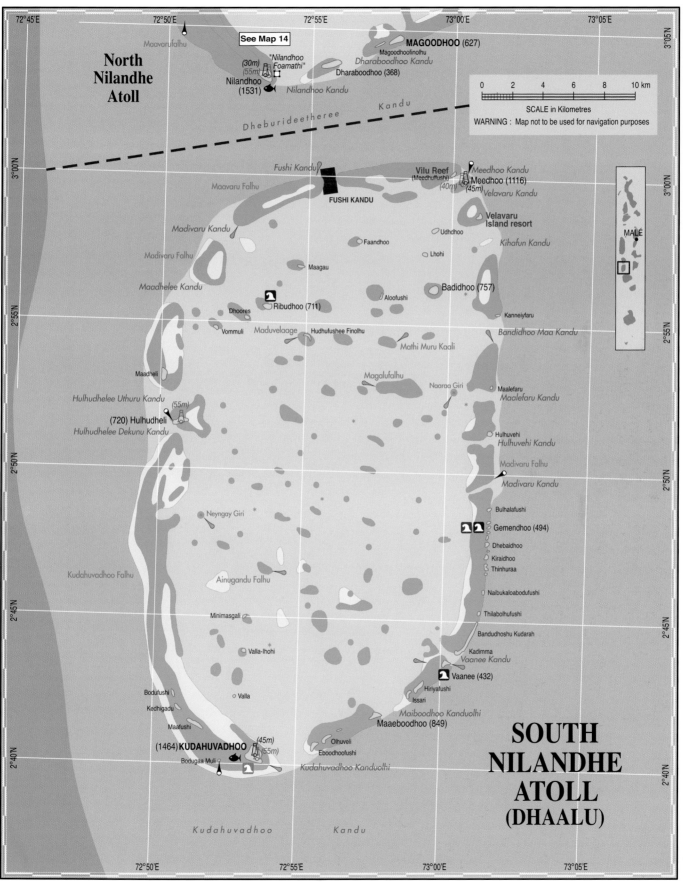

North Nilandhe Atoll

72°45'E 72°50'E 72°55'E 73°00'E 73°05'E

Maavarufalhu

See Map 14

(30m)
(55m) "Nilandhoo Foamathi"
Nilandhoo (1531)

MAGOODHOO (627)
Magoodhoofinolhu
Dharaboodhoo Kandu
Dharaboodhoo (368)

Nilandhoo Kandu

Dheburideetheree   Kandu

Fushi Kandu

Maavaru Falhu

FUSHI KANDU

Vilu Reef (Meedhuffushi)
(40m)
Meedhoo (1116) *(45m)*
Meedhoo Kandu
Velavaru Kandu

Velavaru Island resort

Madivaru Kandu

Madivaru Falhu

Faandhoo
Udhdhoo
Kihafun Kandu

Lhohi

Maagau

Maadhelee Kandu

Aloofushi
Badidhoo (757)

Dhoores
Ribudhoo (711)

Vommuli
Maduvelaage
Hudhufushee Finolhu

Kanneiyfaru

Bandidhoo Maa Kandu

Mathi Muru Kaali

Maadheli

Hulhudhelee Uthuru Kandu

(55m)
(720) Hulhudheli
Hulhudhelee Dekunu Kandu

Magalufalhu

Naaraa Giri

Maalefaru
Maalefaru Kandu

Hulhuvehi
Hulhuvehi Kandu

Neyngay Giri

Kudahuvadhoo Falhu

Ainugandu Falhu

Madivaru Falhu
Madivaru Kandu

Bulhalafushi
Gemendhoo (494)
Dhebaidhoo
Kiraidhoo
Thinhuraa

Naibukaloabodufushi

Thilabolhufushi

Minimasgali

Bandudhoshu Kudarah
Kadimma
Vaanee Kandu

Valla-lhohi

Vaanee (432)

Bodufushi
Kedhigadu

Valla

Hiriyafushi
Issari

Maiboodhoo Kanduolhi
Maaeboodhoo (849)

Maafushi

(45m)
(1464) KUDAHUVADHOO *(55m)*
Bodugaa Muli

Olhuveli
Eboodhoofushi

Kudahuvadhoo Kanduolhi

Kudahuvadhoo   Kandu

SOUTH NILANDHE ATOLL (DHAALU)

MALÉ

0 2 4 6 8 10 km

SCALE in Kilometres

WARNING : Map not to be used for navigation purposes

3°05'N

3°00'N

2°55'N

2°50'N

2°45'N

2°40'N

MAP 16

MULAKU
ATOLL
(MEEMU)

Vattaru Kandu

Mulaku Kandu

Fenboafinolhu

Gonifalhu Muli

Gaahuraa
Vanhuravalhi Kandu

Olhugandu

Raabandhihuraa

Aiydhoshu Beyru Giri

Dhigugiri
Dhiggaru (1175)
Fathassaagiri
Maduvvari (659)

(80m)
Diggaru Kandu
Maduvvari Kandu

Raiymandhoo (220)
(45m)

Madifushi (201)

Erruh-huraa

Veriheiybe

Uthuruboduveli

Hurasveli

Kahlhu Giri

Rayvilla Wreck

(1424) Boli Mulah
(40m)

Veyvah (268)

HAKURA THILA
(Lhazikuraadi)

Mulah Kandu

Mulee Kandu

Boahuraa

MULI (759)

*Prazer E Allegria,
March 17, 1844*

Maalhaveli

(50m)
Naalaafushi (464)

Medhufushi Island Resort

Gongalu Huraa

Seedhihuraa

Seedhihuraa Veligandu

Thuvaru

Thuvarudhekunu Kandu

Maabadheethun

Kekuraalhuveli

Chaaya Lagoon Hakuraa Huraa
(Hakuraahuraa)

Gasveli (Proposed Resort)
Dhekunuboduveli (Proposed Resort)
Kudausfushi (Proposed Resort)

Kudahini Kandu

Maausfushi
Maahuraa
Fenfuraaveli

Haafushi
(85m)

Kurali
Kuradhigandu

(72m)

Kolhufushi (1213)

Dhiththudi
*Kalhuohfummi,
1573*

Kurali Kandu

Kudahuvadhoo Kandu

MALÉ

| 0 | 2 | 4 | 6 | 8 | 10 km |

SCALE in Kilometres

WARNING : Map not to be used for navigation purposes

Hataru   Alholhu   Medu

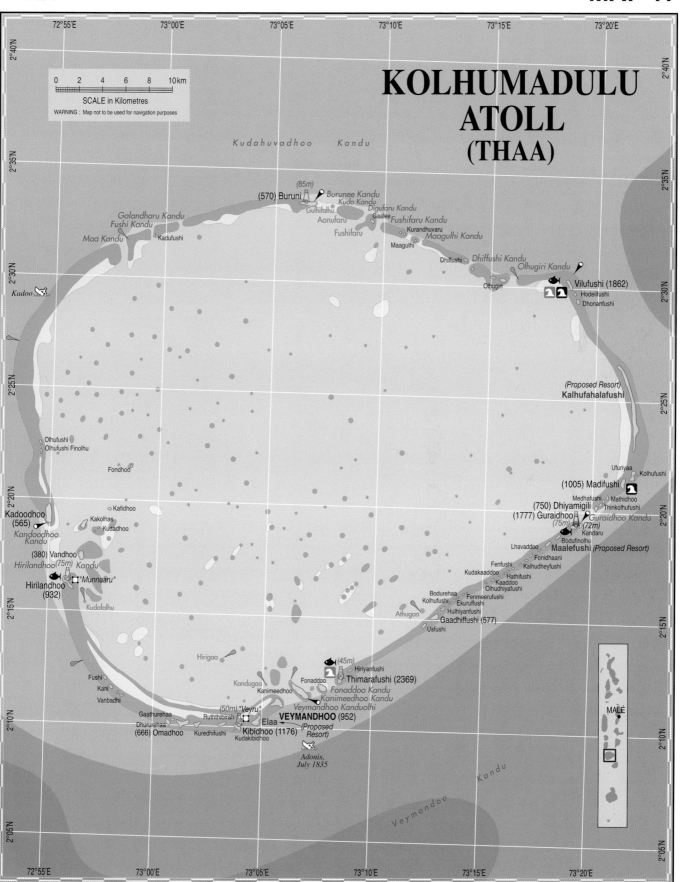

KOLHUMADULU ATOLL (THAA)

Scale: 0 2 4 6 8 10km
SCALE in Kilometres
WARNING : Map not to be used for navigation purposes

Kudahuvadhoo Kandu

(85m)
(570) Buruni
Burunee Kandu
Kuda Kandu
Gulhifalhu
Digufaru Kandu
Aanufaru
Gaalee *Fushifaru Kandu*
Galandharu Kandu
Fushi Kandu
Fushifaru
Kurandhuvaru
Maagulhi Kandu
Maa Kandu
Kadufushi
Maagulhi
Dhiffushi *Dhiffushi Kandu*
Olhugiri Kandu
Olhugiri
Kadoo
Vilufushi (1862)
Hodelifushi
Dhonanfushi

(Proposed Resort)
Kalhufahalafushi

Olhufushi
Olhufushi Finolhu

Ufuriyaa
Kolhufushi
Fondhoo
(1005) Madifushi
Medhafushi Mathidhoo
Kafidhoo
(750) Dhiyamigili Thinkolhufushi
Kadoodhoo
(565)
Kakolhas
Kudadhoo
(1777) Guraidhoo *Guraidhoo Kandu*
(75m) *(72m)*
Kandoodhoo
Kandu
Kandaru
(380) Vandhoo
Bodufinolhu
Hirilandhoo *(75m)* *Kandu*
Lhavaddoo **Maalefushi** *(Proposed Resort)*
Hirilandhoo
(932) □ *"Munnaaru"*
Fonidhaani
Fenfushi Kalhudheyfushi
Kudafalhu
Kudakaaddoo Hathifushi
Kaaddoo
Olhudhiyafushi
Bodurehaa Fenmeerufushi
Kolhufushi Ekuruffushi
Hulhiyanfushi
Athugaa **Gaadhiffushi (577)**
Usfushi

Hirigaa

(45m)
Hiriyanfushi
Fushi
Fonaddoo **Thimarafushi (2369)**
Kani Kandugaa
Vanbadhi Kanimeedhoo *Fonaddoo Kandu*
Kanimeedhoo Kandu
(50m) "Veyru" *Veymandhoo Kanduolhi*
Gaathurehaa Ruththibirah □ **VEYMANDHOO (952)**
Dhururehaa **Elaa** *(Proposed*
(666) Omadhoo Kuredhifushi **Kibidhoo (1176)** *Resort)*
Kudakibidhoo

Adonis,
July 1835

Veymandoo Kandu

MALÉ

MAP 18

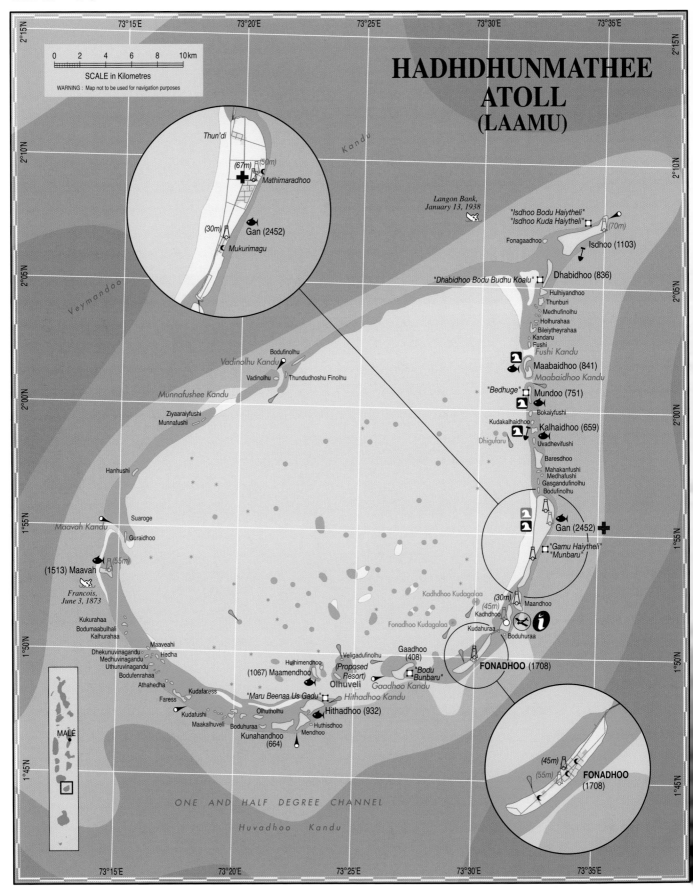

SCALE in Kilometres

WARNING : Map not to be used for navigation purposes

HADHDHUNMATHEE ATOLL (LAAMU)

Thun'di

(67m) (50m)

Mathimaradhoo

(30m) Gan (2452)

Mukurimagu

Kandu

Langon Bank,
January 13, 1938

"Isdhoo Bodu Haiytheli"
"Isdhoo Kuda Haiytheli" (70m)

Fonagaadhoo Isdhoo (1103)

"Dhabidhoo Bodu Budhu Koalu" Dhabidhoo (836)

Hulhiyandhoo
Thunburi
Medhufinolhu
Holhurahaa
Bileiytheyrahaa
Kandaru
Fushi *Fushi Kandu*

Maabaidhoo (841)
Maabaidhoo Kandu

"Bedhuge" Mundoo (751)

Bokaiyfushi

Kudakalhaidhoo Kalhaidhoo (659)

Uvadhevifushi

Baresdhoo
Mahakanfushi
Medhafushi
Gasgandufinolhu
Bodufinolhu

Veymandoo

Bodufinolhu
Vadinolhu Kandu

Vadinolhu Thundudhoshu Finolhu

Munnafushee Kandu

Ziyaaraiyfushi
Munnafushi

Dhigufaru

Gan (2452)

"Gamu Haiytheli"
"Munbaru"

Hanhushi

(30m) Maandhoo
Kadhdhoo Kudagalaa (45m) Kadhdhoo

Suaroge

Guraidhoo

Maavah Kandu

Fonadhoo Kudagalaa

Kudahuraa

Boduhuraa

(1513) Maavah (55m)

*Francois,
June 3, 1873*

FONADHOO (1708)

Kukurahaa
Bodumaabulhali
Kalhurahaa

Maaveahi
Hedha

Dhekunuvinagandu
Medhuvinagandu
Uthuruvinagandu
Bodufenrahaa

Hulhimendhoo

Gaadhoo (408)

"Bodu Bunbaru"

Veligadufinolhu

(1067) Maamendhoo (Proposed Resort)

Olhuveli

Athahedha

Kudafaress

Faress

"Maru Beenaa Us Gadu"

Gaadhoo Kandu

Hithadhoo Kandu

Olhutholhu Hithadhoo (932)

Kudafushi

Maakalhuveli

Boduhuraa

Huthisdhoo
Mendhoo

Kunahandhoo (664)

(45m)

(55m) FONADHOO (1708)

MALÉ

ONE AND HALF DEGREE CHANNEL

Huvadhoo Kandu

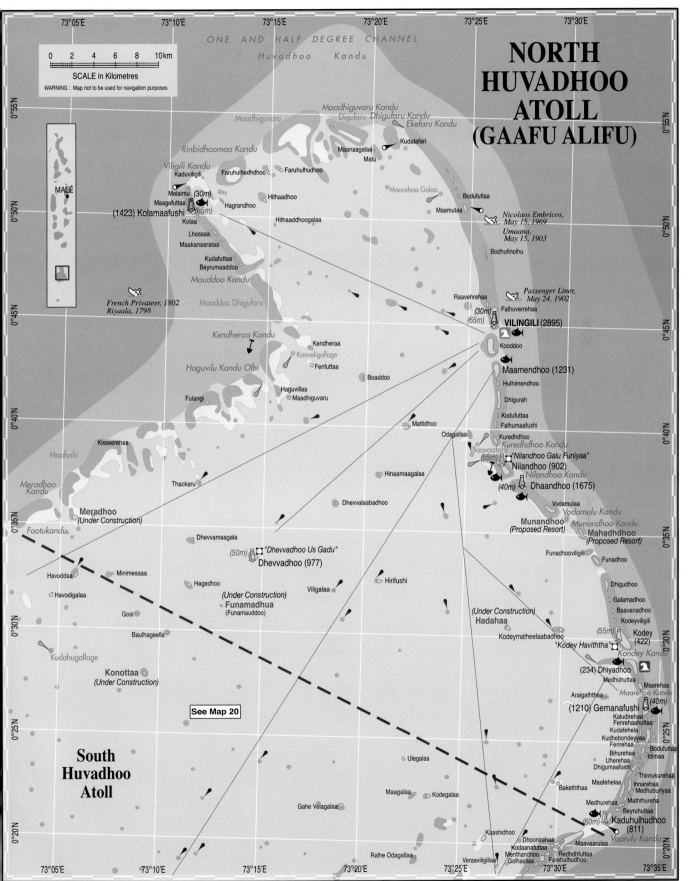

ONE AND HALF DEGREE CHANNEL

Huvadhoo Kandu

NORTH HUVADHOO ATOLL (GAAFU ALIFU)

0 2 4 6 8 10km

SCALE in Kilometres

WARNING : Map not to be used for navigation purposes

MALÉ

Maadhiguvaru Kandu

Maadhiguvaru

Digufaru *Dhigufaru Kandu*

Ekefaru Kandu

Kudalafari

Rinbidhoomaa Kandu

Maanaagalaa

Matu

Viligili Kandu

Kaduviligili

Faruhulhedhdhoo

Faruhulhudhoo

Melaimu *(30m)*

Maarehaa Galaa

Hithaadhoo

Maagefuttaa *(65m)*

Hagrandhoo

Boduftaa

(1423) Kolamaafushi

Kolaa

Hithaaddhoogalaa

Maamutaa

Lhossaa

Maakanaarataa

Nicolaos Embricos, May 15, 1969

Umaana, May 15, 1903

Kudafuttaa

Beyrumaaddoo

Bodhufinolhu

Mauddoo Kandu

Maaddoo Dhigufaru

Raavehrrehaa

Passenger Liner, May 24, 1902

Falhuverrehaa

French Privateer, 1802
Riyaala, 1798

(30m)

(65m) VILINGILI (2895)

Kendheraa Kandu

Kendheraa

Kooddoo

Kanneligallage

Fenfuttaa

Maamendhoo (1231)

Haguvilu Kandu Olhi

Hulhimendhoo

Boaddoo

Dhigurah

Fulangi

Haguvillaa

Maadhiguvaru

Koduftaa

Falhumaafushi

Mattidhoo

Odagallaa

Kuredhdhoo

Boavaataru *Kuredhdhoo Kandu*

Kisseerehaa

(55m) "Nilandhoo Galu Funiyaa"

Maafushi

Nilandhoo (902)

Nilandhoo Kandu

Thackaru

Hinaamaagalaa

(40m) Dhaandhoo (1675)

Meradhoo Kandu

Dhevvalaabadhoo

Vodamulaa

Vodamulu Kandu

Munandhoo *(Proposed Resort)*

Munandhoo Kandu

Meradhoo *(Under Construction)*

Mahadhdhoo *(Proposed Resort)*

Footukandu

Dhevvamaagala

Funadhooviligili

Funadhoo

(50m) "Dhevvadhoo Us Gadu"

Dhevvadhoo (977)

Dhigudhoo

Havoddaa

Minimessaa

Hagedhoo

(Under Construction) Funamadhua *(Funamauddoo)*

Viligalaa

Hirifushi

Galamadhoo

Havodigalaa

Baavanadhoo

Kodeyviligili

Gosi

(55m) Kodey *(422)*

Kudahugallage

Baulhageella

Kodeymatheelaabadhoo

"Kodey Haviththa"

Kondey Kandu

Konottaa *(Under Construction)*

(Under Construction) Hadahaa

(234) Dhiyadhoo

See Map 20

Medhuhuttaa

Maarehaa

Araigaththaa

Maarehaa Kandu

(40m)

South Huvadhoo Atoll

(1210) Gemanafushi

Kaludirehaa

Fenrehaahuttaa

Kudafehela

Kudhebondeyyaa

Fenrehaa

Boduftaa

Ulegalaa

Bihurehaa

Idimaa

Uherehaa

Dhigumaafushi

Thinrukurehaa

Bakeththaa

Maafehelaa

Innarehaa

Medhuburiyaa

Maagalaa

Kodegalaa

Medhurehaa

Maththurehaa

Beyruhuttaa

Gahe Velagalaa

(60m) Kaduhulhudhoo *(811)*

Kaashidhoo

Vaarulu Kandu

Dhoonirehaa

Kodaanafuttaa

Menthandhoo

Redhdhfuttaa

Ralhe Odagallaa

Veraaviligillaa

Golhaallaa

Farehulhudhoo

MAP 20

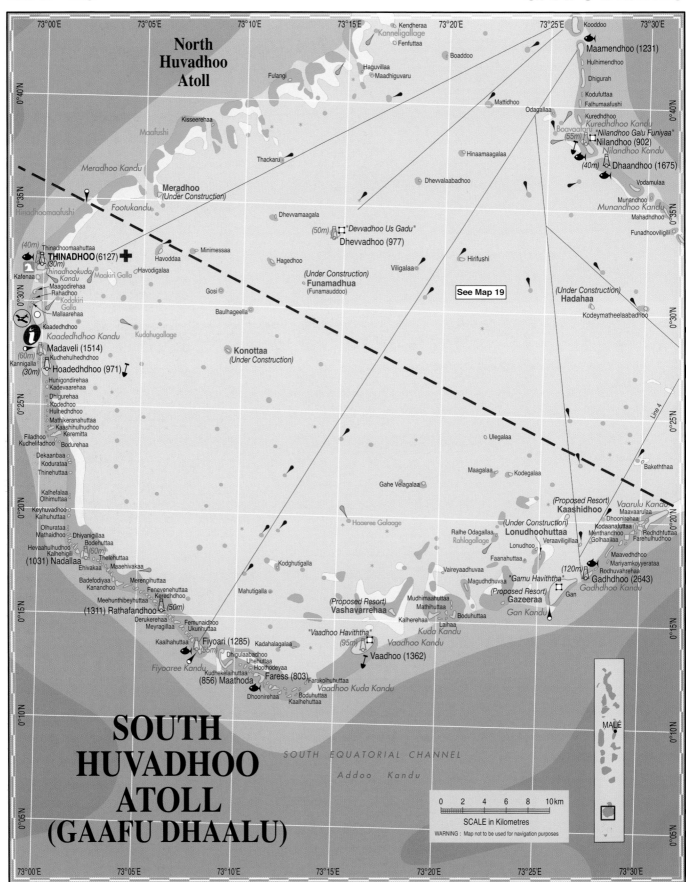

North Huvadhoo Atoll

Kanneligallage
Kendheraa
Fenfuttaa
Boaddoo
Haguvillaa
Maadhiguvaru
Fulangi
Kisseerehaa
Maafushi
Thackaru
Maadhiguvaru
Mattidhoo
Odagallaa
Hinaamaagalaa
Dhewalaabadhoo

Kooddoo
Maamendhoo (1231)
Hulhimendhoo
Dhigurah
Kodufuttaa
Falhumaafushi
Kuredhdhoo
Kuredhdhoo Kandu
Boavaataru *"Nilandhoo Galu Funiyaa"*
(55m) Nilandhoo (902)
Nilandhoo Kandu
(40m) Dhaandhoo (1675)
Vodamulaa
Munandhoo
Munandhoo Kandu
Mahadhdhoo
Funadhooviligili

Meradhoo Kandu
Meradhoo *(Under Construction)*
Hinadhoomaafushi *Footukandu*
Dhevvamaagala
(50m) *"Devvadhoo Us Gadu"*
Dhevvadhoo (977)

(40m) Thinadhoomaahuttaa
THINADHOO (6127)
(30m)
Kafenaa
Thinadhookuda Kandu *Maakiri Galla*
Maagodirehaa
Rahadhoo
Kodakiri Galla
Mallaarehaa
Kaadedhdhoo
Kaadedhdhoo Kandu
Havoddaa
Minimessaa
Havodigalaa
Hagedhoo
Gosi

Kudahugallage
Baulhageella

Hirifushi
Viligalaa

See Map 19

(Under Construction)
Funamadhua
(Funamauddoo)

(Under Construction)
Hadahaa
Kodeymatheelaabadhoo

Madaveli (1514)
Kudhehulhedhdhoo
(60m)
Kannigalla
(30m) Hoadedhdhoo (971)
Hunigondirehaa
Kadevaarehaa
Dhigurehaa
Kodedhoo
Hulhedhdhoo
Mathikeranahuttaa
Kaashihulhudhoo
Keremitta
Filadhoo
Kudhelifadhoo
Bodurehaa
Dekaanbaa
Kodurataa
Thinehuttaa
Kalhefalaa
Olhimuttaa
Keyhuvadhoo
Kalhurihuttaa
Olhurataa
Mathaidhoo
Hevaahulhudhoo
Dhiyanigillaa
Kalhehigili
Bodehuttaa
(60m)
(1031) Nadallaa
Thelehuttaa
Ehivakaa
Maaehivakaa
Badefodiyaa
Merengihuttaa
Kanandhoo
Fenevenehuttaa
Meehunthibeyhuttaa
Keredhdhoo
(1311) Rathafandhoo
(50m)
Derukerehaa
Femunaidhoo
Meyragillaa
Ukurihuttaa
Kaalhahuttaa
Fiyoari (1285)
(55m)
Fiyoaree Kandu
Kudhekelaihuttaa
(856) Maathoda
Dhoonirehaa

Konottaa
(Under Construction)

Ulegalaa

Bakeththaa

Maagalaa
Kodegalaa
Gahe Velagalaa

(Proposed Resort)
Kaashidhoo
Vaarulu Kandu
Maavaarulaa
Dhoonirehaa
Kodaanaluttaa
Menthandhoo
Redhdhfhuttaa
Golhaalaa
Farehulhudhoo
(Under Construction)
Lonudhoohuttaa
Veraaviligillaa
Lonudhoo
Ralhe Odagallaa
Rahlagallage
Faanahuttaa
Maavedhdhoo
Mariyamkoyyerataa
(120m)
Rodhuvarehaa
Gadhdhoo (2643)
Gadhdhoo Kandu
Vaireyaadhuvaa
Magudhdhuvaa
"Gamu Haviththa"
Gan
(Proposed Resort)
Gazeeraa
Gan Kandu
Mudhimaahuttaa
Mathihuttaa
Boduhuttaa
Kalherehaa
Laihaa
Kuda Kandu

Haaeree Galaage

Kodghutigalla

Mahutigalla

(Proposed Resort)
Vashavarrehaa

"Vaadhoo Haviththa"
(95m)
Vaadhoo (1362)

Kadahalagalaa
Dhigulaabadhoo
Uhehuttaa
Hoothodeyaa
Faress (803)
Farukolhuhuttaa
Boduhuttaa
Kaalhehuttaa
Vaadhoo Kuda Kandu
Vaadhoo Kandu

Line 4

SOUTH HUVADHOO ATOLL (GAAFU DHAALU)

SOUTH EQUATORIAL CHANNEL
Addoo Kandu

MALÉ

```
0   2   4   6   8   10 km
```
SCALE in Kilometres
WARNING : Map not to be used for navigation purposes

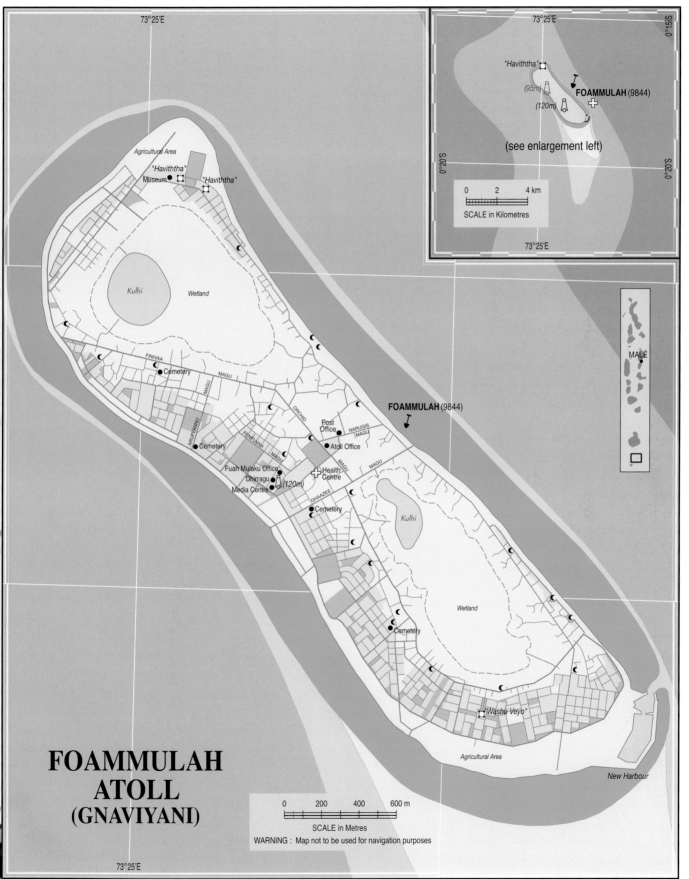

73°25'E

"Haviththa"
(95m)
FOAMMULAH (9844)
(120m)

(see enlargement left)

0   2   4 km
SCALE in Kilometres

73°25'E

Agricultural Area

"Haviththa"
Museum
"Haviththa"

Kulhi   Wetland

FINIVAA

MAGU

Cemetery

MAGU

IMAGU

ORCHID

ARIUFANNU

Cemetery

FENFUVAH

MAGU

NARUGIS MAGU

Post Office

Atoll Office

Fuah Mulaku Office

Dhirragu
Media Centre

(120m)

Health Centre

MAGU

MAGU

GHAAZEE

Cemetery

FOAMMULAH (9844)

Kulhi

Wetland

Cemetery

MALÉ

"Washu Veyo"

Agricultural Area

New Harbour

FOAMMULAH
ATOLL
(GNAVIYANI)

0   200   400   600 m
SCALE in Metres

WARNING : Map not to be used for navigation purposes

73°25'E

MAP 22

SEENU

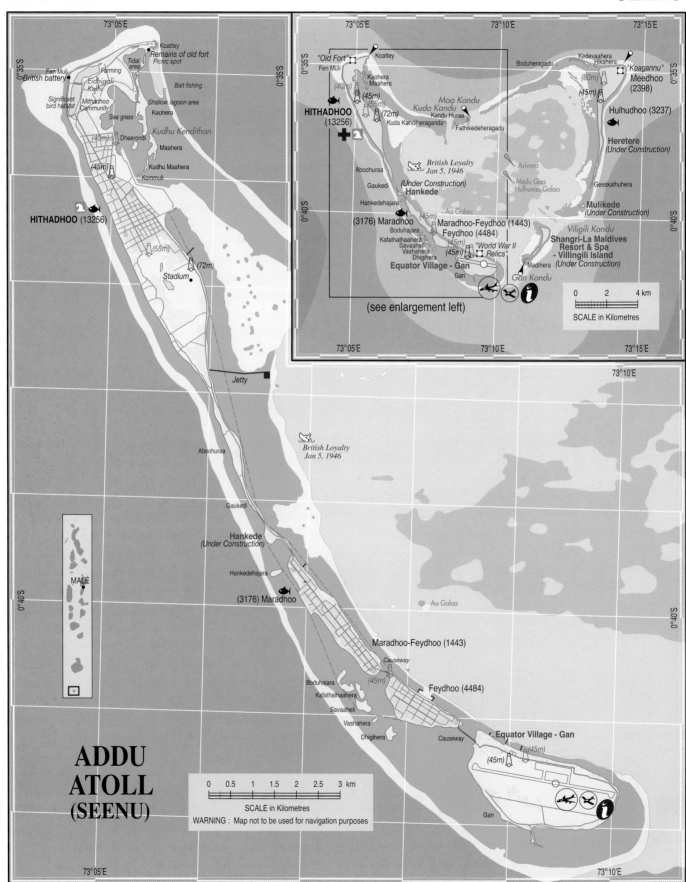

Enlargement (top right)

73°05'E 73°10'E 73°15'E

0°35'S

"Old Fort" Koattey
Fen Muli Kedevaahera
Kaohera Hikahera "Koagannu"
Maahera Boduheragadu Meedhoo
(40m) (80m) (2398)
HITHADHOO (45m) (45m) Hulhudhoo (3237)
(13256) (55m)
(72m) Heretere
Kuda Kandiheraganda (Under Construction)
Maa Kandu
Kuda Kandu
Kandu Huraa
Fathikedeheragadu
Aboohuraa Arivara
British Loyalty
Jan 5, 1946 Medu Gaa
Gaukedi (Under Construction) Hulhuvaa Galaa Gesskalhuhera
Hankede
Hankedehajara Mulikede
(45m) (Under Construction)
Aa Galaa
(3176) Maradhoo Maradhoo-Feydhoo (1443) Viligili Kandu
Boduhajara Feydhoo (4484) Shangri-La Maldives
Kafathalhaahera (45m) Resort & Spa
Savaaheli (45m) "World War II - Villingili Island
Vashahera Relics" (Under Construction)
Dhigihera Madihera
Equator Village - Gan Gan Kandu
Gan

(see enlargement left)

0 2 4 km
SCALE in Kilometres

0°40'S

73°05'E 73°10'E 73°15'E

Main map (left)

73°05'E

0°35'S

Koattey
Remains of old fort
Picnic spot
Fen Muli
British battery Tidal
area
Eidhigali Farming
Kulhi
Significant Bait fishing
bird habitat Mithadhoo
Community Shallow lagoon area
Sea grass Kaohera
Kudhu Kendithan
(40m)
Dheerondi
Maahera
(45m) Kudhu Maahera
Kommuli

HITHADHOO (13256)

(55m)

(72m)

Stadium

Jetty

Aboohuraa

British Loyalty
Jan 5, 1946

Gaukedi

Hankede
(Under Construction)

Hankedehajara

(3176) Maradhoo

Maradhoo-Feydhoo (1443)

Causeway
(45m)

Boduhajara
Kafathalhaahera Feydhoo (4484)
Savaaheli
Vashahera Causeway
Dhigihera Equator Village - Gan
(45m)
(45m)
Gan

MALÉ

ADDU ATOLL (SEENU)

0 0.5 1 1.5 2 2.5 3 km

SCALE in Kilometres

WARNING : Map not to be used for navigation purposes

73°05'E 73°10'E

Index

ISLAND NAME	ATOLL	MAP #	REFERENCE		ISLAND NAME	ATOLL	MAP #	REFERENCE	
Aarah (U)	Kaafu	9	4°14'N	73°29'E	Boaddoo (U)	Gaafu Alifu	19	0°43'N	73°20'E
Aarah (U)	Raa	6	5°27'N	72°57'E	Boahuraa (U)	Meemu	16	2°56'N	73°36'E
Aarah (U)	Vaavu	13	3°30'N	73°32'E	Bodehuttaa (U)	Gaafu Dhaalu	20	0°18'N	73°02'E
Aboohuraa (U)	Seenu	22	0°38'S	73°06'E	Bodhufinolhu (U)	Gaafu Alifu	19	0°49'N	73°26'E
Adhangau (U)	Faafu	14	3°08'N	73°01'E	Bodubados (R)	Kaafu	9	4°17'N	73°29'E
Adonis (Wk)	Thaa	17	2°10'N	73°12'E	Bodufaahuraa (U)	Lhaviyani	8	5°19'N	73°39'E
Agolhitheemu (I)	Raa	6	5°48'N	73°01'E	Bodufarufinolhu (U)	Raa	6	5°31'N	72°48'E
Ahivahfushi (U)	Baa	7	5°14'N	72°52'E	Bodufenmaaeboodhoo (U)	Raa	6	5°38'N	72°56'E
Aidhoo (U)	Baa	7	5°12'N	73°10'E	Bodufenrahaa (U)	Laamu	18	1°49'N	73°17'E
Akirifushi (U)	Kaafu	9	4°38'N	73°29'E	Bodufinolhu (U)	Alifu Dhaalu	12	3°29'N	72°47'E
Alidhoo (PR)	Haa Alifu	1	6°52'N	73°09'E	Bodufinolhu (U)	Baa	7	5°01'N	72°52'E
Alidhuffarufinolhu (U)	Haa Alifu	1	6°52'N	73°06'E	Bodufinolhu (U)	Kaafu	10	3°52'N	73°28'E
Alifushi (I)	Raa	6	5°57'N	72°57'E	Bodufinolhu (U)	Laamu	18	2°02'N	73°23'E
Aligau (U)	Lhaviyani	8	5°15'N	73°31'E	Bodufinolhu (U)	Laamu	18	1°57'N	73°33'E
Alikoirah (U)	Alifu Alifu	11	3°57'N	72°53'E	Bodufinolhu (U)	Thaa	17	2°19'N	73°18'E
Alimathaa (R)	Vaavu	13	3°36'N	73°29'E	Bodufolhudhoo (I)	Alifu Alifu	11	4°11'N	72°47'E
Aloofushi (U)	Dhaalu	15	2°56'N	72°58'E	Bodufushi (U)	Dhaalu	15	2°43'N	72°51'E
Al Kareem (Wk)	Alifu Dhaalu	12	3°37'N	72°58'E	Bodufushi (U)	Noonu	5	5°43'N	73°25'E
Anantara Maldives (R)	Kaafu	10	3°58'N	73°30'E	Bodufushi (U)	Raa	6	5°31'N	72°58'E
Anbaraa (U)	Vaavu	13	3°23'N	73°26'E	Bodufuttaa (U)	Gaafu Alifu	19	0°51'N	73°24'E
Angaagau (U)	Alifu Dhaalu	12	3°39'N	72°49'E	Bodufuttaa (U)	Gaafu Alifu	19	0°25'N	73°35'E
Angaga (R)	Alifu Dhaalu	12	3°39'N	72°49'E	Bodugaa Muli (U)	Dhaalu	15	2°40'N	72°52'E
Anhenunfushi (U)	Baa	7	5°21'N	72°58'E	Bodugaahuraa (U)	Lhaviyani	8	5°22'N	73°39'E
Angsana (R)	Kaafu	9	4°18'N	73°25'E	Boduhaiykodi (U)	Raa	6	5°37'N	72°59'E
Aracan (Wk)	Kaafu	9	4°45'N	73°35'E	Boduhajara (U)	Seenu	22	0°41'S	73°07'E
Araigaththaa (U)	Gaafu Alifu	19	0°27'N	73°32'E	Boduheragadu (U)	Seenu	22	0°35'S	73°12'E
Arilundhoo (U)	Raa	6	5°39'N	72°58'E	Boduhithi (U)	Kaafu	9	4°26'N	73°23'E
Ariyadhoo (U)	Alifu Dhaalu	12	3°28'N	72°52'E	Boduhuraa (I)	Raa	6	5°26'N	73°0'E
Asdhoo (U)	Kaafu	9	4°28'N	73°39'E	Boduhuraa (R)	Kaafu	10	3°58'N	73°31'E
Asdu (R)	Kaafu	9	4°28'N	73°39'E	Boduhuraa (U)	Laamu	18	1°47'N	73°21'E
Athahedha (U)	Laamu	18	1°48'N	73°17'E	Boduhuraa (U)	Laamu	18	1°51'N	73°32'E
Athurugau (R)	Alifu Dhaalu	12	3°53'N	72°49'E	Bodhuhuraa (U)	Lhaviyani	8	5°24'N	73°39'E
Baarah (I)	Haa Alifu	1	6°49'N	73°12'E	Boduhuttaa (U)	Gaafu Dhaalu	20	0°12'N	73°13'E
Baavanadhoo (U)	Gaafu Alifu	19	0°32'N	73°32'E	Boduhuttaa (U)	Gaafu Dhaalu	20	0°15'N	73°21'E
Badaidhidhdhoo (U)	Noonu	5	5°41'N	73°16'E	Bodukaashihuraa (U)	Alifu Dhaalu	12	3°53'N	72°58'E
Badaveri (U)	Raa	6	5°37'N	72°52'E	Bodulhaimendhoo (U)	Noonu	5	6°00'N	73°18'E
Badefodiyaa (U)	Gaafu Dhaalu	20	0°17'N	73°04'E	Bodumaabulhali (U)	Laamu	18	1°51'N	73°16'E
Badidhoo (I)	Dhaalu	15	2°56'N	72°59'E	Bodumohoraa (U)	Vaavu	13	3°21'N	73°32'E
Bahurukabeeru (U)	Lhaviyani	8	5°23'N	73°24'E	Bodunaagoashi (U)	Haa Dhaalu	3	6°40'N	72°53'E
Bakeththaa (U)	Gaafu Alifu	19	0°23'N	73°30'E	Bodurehaa (U)	Gaafu Dhaalu	20	0°23'N	73°01'E
Banana Reef (P)	Kaafu	9	4°15'N	73°32'E	Bodurehaa (U)	Thaa	17	2°16'N	73°14'E
Bandiduffushi (U)	Faafu	14	3°09'N	72°56'E	Boifushi (U)	Baa	7	5°18'N	72°59'E
Bandos (R)	Kaafu	9	4°17'N	73°29'E	Bokaiyfushi (U)	Laamu	18	2°00'N	73°32'E
Bandudhoshu Kudarah (U)	Dhaalu	15	2°45'N	73°02'E	Boli Mulah (I)	Meemu	16	2°57'N	73°35'E
Banyan Tree (R)	Kaafu	9	4°18'N	73°26'E	Bolifushi (R)	Kaafu	10	4°06'N	73°24'E
Baresdhoo (U)	Laamu	18	1°58'N	73°33'E	Bolifushi (Wk)	Kaafu	10	4°06'N	73°24'E
Baros Island Resort (R)	Kaafu	9	4°16'N	73°27'E	Bomasdhoo (U)	Noonu	5	5°58'N	73°21'E
Baros Maldives (R)	Kaafu	9	4°17'N	73°26'E	British Loyalty (Wk)	Seenu	21	0°42'S	73°07'E
Bathala (R)	Alifu Alifu	11	4°04'N	72°58'E	Bulhaahohi (U)	Alifu Dhaalu	12	3°44'N	72°44'E
Bathalaa (U)	Baa	7	5°22'N	73°04'E	Bulhalafushi (U)	Dhaalu	15	2°49'N	73°02'E
Baulhageella (U)	Gaafu Dhaalu	20	0°30'N	73°10'E	Burehifasdhoo (U)	Noonu	5	5°58'N	73°22'E
Beenaafushi (U)	Haa Alifu	1	6°56'N	73°08'E	Buruni (I)	Thaa	17	2°34'N	73°06'E
Berimmadhoo (I)	Haa Alifu	1	7°03'N	72°58'E	Captain Pentalis (Wk)	Haa Alifu	1	6°53'N	73°14'E
Beyruhuttaa (U)	Gaafu Alifu	19	0°22'N	73°33'E	Cinnamon Resort & Spa (R)	Haa Alifu	1	6°51'N	73°09'E
Beyrumaaddoo (U)	Gaafu Alifu	19	0°48'N	73°13'E	Citomo (Wk)	Alifu Alifu	11	4°00'N	72°57'E
Bihurehaa (U)	Gaafu Alifu	19	0°25'N	73°34'E	Clan Alpine (Wk)	Kaafu	9	4°45'N	73°35'E
Biledhdhoo (I)	Faafu	14	3°07'N	72°59'E	Club Med Farukolufushi (R)	Kaafu	9	4°14'N	73°33'E
Bileffahi (I)	Shaviyani	4	6°20'N	72°58'E	Club Med Kanifinolhu (R)	Kaafu	9	4°21'N	73°36'E
Bileiytheyrahaa (U)	Laamu	18	2°03'N	73°32'E	Club Rannalhi	Kaafu	10	3°54'N	73°22'E
Bis Huraa (U)	Shaviyani	4	6°09'N	73°18'E	Coco Palm Bodu Hithi (R)	Kaafu	9	4°26'N	73°25'E
Biyaadhoo (U)	Kaafu	10	3°56'N	73°27'E	Coco Palm Dhunikolhu (R)	Baa	7	5°03'N	72°53'E
Biyadoo (R)	Kaafu	10	3°56'N	73°27'E	Coco Palm Kuda Hithu (R)	Kaafu	9	4°25'N	73°25'E

(PR) - Proposed Resort   (R) - Resort   (U) - Uninhabited Island   (I) - Inhabited Island   (WK) - Wreck   (P) - Protected Marine Area

ISLAND NAME	ATOLL	MAP #	REFERENCE		ISLAND NAME	ATOLL	MAP #	REFERENCE
Cocoa Island (R)	Kaafu	10	3°55'N 73°28'E		Dhonanfushi (U)	Thaa	17	2°29'N 73°19'E
Corbin (Wk)	Baa	7	4°54'N 72°56'E		Dhoni Mighili (R)	Alifu Alifu	11	3°57'N 72°55'E
Crusader (Wk)	Kaafu	9	4°45'N 73°35'E		Dhonfanu (I)	Baa	7	5°12'N 73°07'E
Dalsja (Wk)	Kaafu	9	4°12'N 73°31'E		Dhonveli Huraa (U)	Shaviyani	4	6°11'N 73°18'E
Daravandhoo (I)	Baa	7	5°09'N 73°08'E		Dhon Veli (R)	Kaafu	9	4°19'N 73°36'E
Dekaanbaa (U)	Gaafu Dhaalu	20	0°23'N 73°02'E		Dhoonidhoo (U)	Kaafu	9	4°12'N 73°31'E
Dhaandhoo (I)	Gaafu Alifu	19	0°37'N 73°28'E		Dhoonirehaa (U)	Gaafu Dhaalu	20	0°11'N 73°12'E
Dhabidhoo (I)	Laamu	18	2°06'N 73°33'E		Dhoonirehaa (U)	Gaafu Dhaalu	20	0°20'N 73°30'E
Dhakandhoo (U)	Baa	7	5°15'N 72°54'E		Dhoores (U)	Dhaalu	15	2°55'N 72°53'E
Dhandhoo (U)	Baa	7	5°14'N 73°10'E		Dhoragali (U)	Raa	6	5°29'N 73°00'E
Dhangethi (I)	Alifu Dhaalu	12	3°36'N 72°58'E		Dhunikolhu (U)	Baa	7	5°03'N 72°53'E
Dhapparu (U)	Haa Alifu	1	6°55'N 73°14'E		Dhururehaa (U)	Thaa	17	2°10'N 73°01'E
Dhapparu (Wk)	Haa Alifu	1	6°55'N 73°14'E		Dhuvaafaru (U)	Raa	6	5°38'N 73°03'E
Dhapparuhuraa (U)	Haa Alifu	1	6°55'N 73°12'E		Dhuvaafaruhuraa (U)	Raa	6	5°38'N 73°03'E
Dharaboodhoo (I)	Faafu	14	3°04'N 72°56'E		Duras (Wk)	Faafu	14	3°16'N 72°49'E
Dharuma (Wk)	Kaafu	9	4°38'N 73°38'E		Eboodhoo (U)	Alifu Dhaalu	12	3°49'N 72°46'E
Dhebaidhoo (U)	Dhaalu	15	2°48'N 73°02'E		Eboodhoo (U)	Baa	7	5°04'N 72°52'E
Dheburidheythereyvaadhoo(U)	Raa	6	5°24'N 72°59'E		Eboodhoo (U)	Kaafu	10	4°05'N 73°31'E
Dheefuram (U)	Noonu	5	5°53'N 73°19'E		Eboodhoofinolhu (U)	Kaafu	10	4°06'N 73°32'E
Dhehassanu Lonu Bui Huraa(U)	Alifu Dhaalu	12	3°36'N 72°54'E		Eboodhoofushi (U)	Dhaalu	15	2°41'N 72°56'E
Dhekenanfaru (U)	Noonu	5	5°55'N 73°09'E		Ebulufushi (U)	Faafu	14	3°08'N 73°02'E
Dhekunuboduveli (R)	Meemu	16	2°49'N 73°27'E		Edipparufushi (U)	Haa Dhaalu	2	6°18'N 72°38'E
Dhekunuvinagandu (U)	Laamu	18	1°50'N 73°16'E		Ehivakaa (U)	Gaafu Dhaalu	20	0°17'N 73°03'E
Dhelibehuraa (U)	Noonu	5	5°51'N 73°27'E		Ehurah Huraa (U)	Kaafu	10	3°49'N 73°25'E
Dherukerehaa (U)	Gaafu Dhaalu	20	0°15'N 73°07'E		Ekasdhoo (U)	Shaviyani	4	6°04'N 73°17'E
Dhevvadhoo (U)	Gaafu Alifu	19	0°34'N 73°15'E		Ekulhivaru (U)	Noonu	5	5°57'N 73°18'E
Dhevvalaabadhoo (U)	Gaafu Alifu	19	0°36'N 73°19'E		Ekuruffushi (U)	Thaa	17	2°16'N 73°13'E
Dhevvamaagala (U)	Gaafu Alifu	19	0°34'N 73°12'E		Ekurufushi (U)	Raa	6	5°46'N 72°52'E
Dhidhdhoo (I)	Alifu Dhaalu	12	3°29'N 72°53'E		Elaa (PR)	Thaa	17	2°10'N 73°05'E
Dhidhdhoo (I)	Haa Alifu	1	6°54'N 73°07'E		Ellaidhoo (R)	Alifu Alifu	11	4°00'N 72°57'E
Dhidhdhoo (U)	Lhaviyani	8	5°23'N 73°23'E		Embudhoo Kandu (P)	Kaafu	10	4°05'N 73°32'E
Dhidhdhoo Finolhu (U)	Alifu Dhaalu	12	3°30'N 72°54'E		Embudu Village (R)	Kaafu	10	4°05'N 73°31'E
Dhiffushi (I)	Kaafu	9	4°27'N 73°43'E		Equator Village (R)	Seenu	22	0°42'S 73°09'E
Dhiffushi (U)	Alifu Dhaalu	12	3°29'N 72°49'E		Erlangen (Wk)	Kaafu	9	4°47'N 73°27'E
Dhiffushi (U)	Lhaviyani	8	5°23'N 73°38'E		Eriyadhoo (U)	Shaviyani	4	6°06'N 73°17'E
Dhiffushi (U)	Thaa	17	2°31'N 73°14'E		Eriyadu (R)	Kaafu	9	4°35'N 73°25'E
Dhigali (U)	Raa	6	5°28'N 72°57'E		Erruh-huraa (U)	Meemu	16	3°03'N 73°37'E
Dhigali Haa (P)	Baa	7	5°08'N 73°02'E		Etheremadivaru (U)	Alifu Alifu	11	4°07'N 72°56'E
Dhiggaru (I)	Meemu	16	3°07'N 73°34'E		Eththigili (U)	Raa	6	5°58'N 72°56'E
Dhiggiri (R)	Vaavu	13	3°38'N 73°29'E		Eydhafushi (I)	Baa	7	5°06'N 73°04'E
Dhiggiri (U)	Alifu Dhaalu	12	3°52'N 72°55'E		Faadhoo (U)	Lhaviyani	8	5°26'N 73°37'E
Dhigihera (U)	Seenu	22	0°41'S 73°08'E		Faanahuttaa (U)	Gaafu Dhaalu	20	0°18'N 73°24'E
Dhigudhoo (U)	Gaafu Alifu	19	0°33'N 73°32'E		Faandhoo (U)	Dhaalu	15	2°58'N 72°57'E
Dhigufaruhuraa (U)	Haa Alifu	1	6°56'N 72°58'E		Faanuvaahuraa (U)	Faafu	14	3°13'N 72°58'E
Dhigufaruvinagadu (U)	Baa	7	5°22'N 72°59'E		Faarafushi (U)	Raa	6	5°46'N 72°58'E
Dhigulaabadhoo (U)	Gaafu Dhaalu	20	0°13'N 73°09'E		Fainu (I)	Raa	6	5°28'N 73°02'E
Dhigumaafushi (U)	Gaafu Alifu	19	0°24'N 73°34'E		Fainuaadham Huraa (U)	Lhaviyani	8	5°22'N 73°39'E
Dhigurah (I)	Alifu Dhaalu	12	3°32'N 72°56'E		Falhuge Miyaruvani (P)	Kaafu	9	4°11'N 73°26'E
Dhigurah (U)	Gaafu Alifu	19	0°42'N 73°26'E		Falhumaafushi (U)	Gaafu Alifu	19	0°40'N 73°26'E
Dhigurah (U)	Noonu	5	5°44'N 73°22'E		Falhuverrehaa (U)	Gaafu Alifu	19	0°46'N 73°26'E
Dhigu Rah (U)	Shaviyani	4	6°03'N 73°04'E		Farehulhudhoo (U)	Gaafu Dhaalu	20	0°19'N 73°29'E
Dhigurehaa (U)	Gaafu Dhaalu	20	0°25'N 73°00'E		Faress (I)	Gaafu Dhaalu	20	0°12'N 73°12'E
Dhiguvarufinolhu (U)	Faafu	14	3°15'N 73°02'E		Fares (U)	Baa	7	5°14'N 72°53'E
Dhiguvelidhoo (U)	Shaviyani	4	6°02'N 73°05'E		Faress (U)	Laamu	18	1°48'N 73°18'E
Dhikkuredhdhoo (U)	Raa	6	5°34'N 72°57'E		Faridhoo (I)	Haa Dhaalu	3	6°47'N 73°03'E
Dhinnaafushi (U)	Raa	6	5°36'N 72°50'E		Faruhulhedhdhoo (U)	Gaafu Alifu	19	0°52'N 73°15'E
Dhinnolhufinolhu (U)	Alifu Alifu	11	4°07'N 72°44'E		Faruhulhudhoo (U)	Gaafu Alifu	19	0°52'N 73°16'E
Dhirubaafushi (U)	Lhaviyani	8	5°21'N 73°39'E		Farukolhu (U)	Shaviyani	4	6°12'N 73°18'E
Dhiththudi (U)	Meemu	16	2°46'N 73°26'E		Farukolhufunadhoo (I)	Shaviyani	4	6°08'N 73°18'E
Dhiyadhoo (I)	Gaafu Alifu	19	0°29'N 73°33'E		Farukolhufushi (U)	Kaafu	9	4°14'N 73°33'E
Dhiyamigili (I)	Thaa	17	2°20'N 73°20'E		Farukolhuhuttaa (U)	Gaafu Dhaalu	20	0°12'N 73°14'E
Dhiyanigillaa (U)	Gaafu Dhaalu	20	0°19'N 73°02'E		Farumuli (U)	Noonu	5	5°52'N 73°29'E
Dholhiyadhoo (PR)	Shaviyani	4	5°59'N 73°13'E		Fasmendhoo (U)	Raa	6	5°29'N 72°53'E
Dholhiyadhookudarah (U)	Shaviyani	4	5°59'N 73°13'E		Fathilkedeheragadu (U)	Seenu	22	0°37'S 73°08'E
Dhonaerikadoodhoo (U)	Noonu	5	5°39'N 73°19'E		Feevah (I)	Shaviyani	4	6°21'N 73°13'E
Dhonakulhi (U)	Haa Alifu	1	6°51'N 73°04'E		Fehendhoo (I)	Baa	7	4°53'N 72°58'E

(PR) - Proposed Resort   (R) - Resort   (U) - Uninhabited Island   (I) - Inhabited Island   (WK) - Wreck   (P) - Protected Marine Area

ISLAND NAME	ATOLL	MAP #	REFERENCE		ISLAND NAME	ATOLL	MAP #	REFERENCE	
Fehigili (U)	Lhaviyani	8	5°33'N	73°29'E	Furanafushi (U)	Kaafu	9	4°15'N	73°33'E
Felidhoo (I)	Vaavu	13	3°28'N	73°33'E	Furaveri (U)	Raa	6	5°26'N	72°54'E
Felivaru (U)	Lhaviyani	8	5°29'N	73°24'E	Fushifaru (U)	Alifu Alifu	11	4°13'N	72°53'E
Felivaru (U)	Noonu	5	5°50'N	73°18'E	Fushi (U)	Laamu	18	2°03'N	73°32'E
Femunaidhoo (U)	Gaafu Dhaalu	20	0°15'N	73°07'E	Fushi (U)	Thaa	17	2°12'N	72°58'E
Fenboafinolhu (U)	Meemu	16	3°10'N	73°24'E	Fushi Kandu (P)	Dhaalu	15	3°00'N	72°55'E
Fenboahuraa (U)	Haa Dhaalu	2	6°23'N	72°42'E	Fushifaru (U)	Lhaviyani	8	5°29'N	73°31'E
Fenfuttaa (U)	Gaafu Alifu	19	0°43'N	73°17'E	Fushifaru Kandu (P)	Lhaviyani	8	5°29'N	73°31'E
Fenevenehuttaa (U)	Gaafu Dhaalu	20	0°16'N	73°06'E	Fushifarurah (U)	Shaviyani	4	6°24'N	72°56'E
Fenfuraaveli (U)	Meemu	16	2°48'N	73°26'E	Fushivelavaru (U)	Noonu	5	5°50'N	73°12'E
Fenfushi (I)	Alifu Dhaalu	12	3°29'N	72°47'E	Fussfaruhuraa (U)	Vaavu	13	3°35'N	73°19'E
Fenfushi (U)	Raa	6	5°23'N	72°54'E	Gaadhiffushi (I)	Thaa	17	2°15'N	73°13'E
Fenfushi (U)	Thaa	17	2°18'N	73°16'E	Gaadhoo (I)	Laamu	18	1°49'N	73°27'E
Fenmeerufushi (U)	Thaa	17	2°16'N	73°14'E	Gaaerifaru (U)	Lhaviyani	8	5°29'N	73°24'E
Fenrehaa (U)	Gaafu Alifu	19	0°25'N	73°34'E	Gaafaru (I)	Kaafu	9	4°44'N	73°30'E
Fenrehaahuttaa (U)	Gaafu Alifu	19	0°26'N	73°35'E	Gaafaru (Wk)	Lhaviyani	8	5°29'N	73°24'E
Feridhoo (U)	Alifu Alifu	11	4°03'N	72°43'E	Gaafushi (U)	Haa Alifu	1	6°52'N	73°04'E
Fesdu (R)	Alifu Alifu	11	4°01'N	72°48'E	Gaagadufaruhuraa (U)	Baa	7	5°23'N	73°04'E
Fesdu Wreck (Wk)	Alifu Alifu	11	4°00'N	72°47'E	Gaagandu (U)	Alifu Alifu	11	4°14'N	72°52'E
Feydhoo (I)	Seenu	22	0°41'S	73°08'E	Gaahuraa (U)	Meemu	16	3°09'N	73°31'E
Feydhoo (I)	Shaviyani	4	6°22'N	73°03'E	Gaakoshinbi (PR)	Shaviyani	4	6°17'N	73°01'E
Feydhoo Finolhu (U)	Kaafu	9	4°13'N	73°29'E	Gaalee (U)	Thaa	17	2°33'N	73°09'E
Fieeali (I)	Faafu	14	3°17'N	72°59'E	Gaamathikulhudhoo (U)	Haa Alifu	1	7°03'N	72°59'E
Fihalhohi (U)	Kaafu	10	3°53'N	73°22'E	Gaathafushi (U)	Alifu Alifu	11	4°02'N	72°48'E
Fihalhohi (R)	Kaafu	10	3°53'N	73°22'E	Gaathu Giri (P)	Kaafu	9	4°15'N	73°32'E
Filadhoo(U)	Gaafu Dhaalu	20	0°24'N	73°00'E	Gaathurehaa (U)	Thaa	17	2°10'N	73°01'E
Filaidhoo (U)	Raa	6	5°32'N	72°58'E	Gaaudoodhoo (U)	Raa	6	5°45'N	73°01'E
Filitheyo (R)	Faafu	14	3°13'N	73°03'E	Gadhdhoo (I)	Gaafu Dhaalu	20	0°17'N	73°28'E
Filitheyo Kandu (P)	Faafu	14	3°12'N	73°03'E	Gahe Velagalaa (U)	Gaafu Dhaalu	20	0°22'N	73°19'E
Filladhoo (I)	Haa Alifu	1	6°53'N	73°14'E	Galamadhoo (U)	Gaafu Alifu	19	0°33'N	73°32'E
Finey (I)	Haa Dhaalu	3	6°45'N	73°03'E	Gallaidhoo (U)	Shaviyani	4	5°58'N	73°07'E
Finolhoss (U)	Baa	7	5°14'N	73°07'E	Gallandhoo (U)	Haa Alifu	1	6°57'N	72°59'E
Finolhu (U)	Alifu Dhaalu	12	3°33'N	72°52'E	Gan (I)	Laamu	18	1°55'N	73°33'E
Firubaidhoo (I)	Shaviyani	4	6°07'N	73°13'E	Gan (U)	Gaafu Dhaalu	20	0°16'N	73°26'E
Fish Head (P)	Alifu Alifu	11	3°58'N	72°55'E	Gan (U)	Seenu	22	0°42'S	73°09'E
Fiyoari (I)	Gaafu Dhaalu	20	0°13'N	73°08'E	Gangehi (R)	Alifu Alifu	11	4°13'N	72°46'E
Foakaidhoo (I)	Shaviyani	4	6°19'N	73°09'E	Gaathu Giri (P)	Kaafu	9	4°15'N	73°32'E
Foammulah (I)	Gnaviyani	21	0°17'S	73°25'E	Gasfinolhu (R)	Kaafu	9	4°22'N	73°38'E
Fodhdhipparu (U)	Noonu	5	5°45'N	73°12'E	Gasgandufinolhu (U)	Laamu	18	1°57'N	73°33'E
Fodhdhoo (I)	Noonu	5	5°44'N	73°13'E	Gasveli (PR)	Meemu	16	2°50'N	73°28'E
Fonaddoo (U)	Thaa	17	2°12'N	73°08'E	Gaukedi (U)	Seenu	22	0°39'S	73°06'E
Fonadhoo (I)	Laamu	18	1°50'N	73°30'E	Gazeeraa (PR)	Gaafu Dhaalu	20	0°16'N	73°24'E
Fonagaadhoo (U)	Laamu	18	2°07'N	73°33'E	Gemanafushi (I)	Gaafu Alifu	19	0°27'N	73°34'E
Fondhoo (U)	Thaa	17	2°21'N	72°59'E	Gemendhoo (I)	Dhaalu	15	2°48'N	73°02'E
Fondidhaani (U)	Thaa	17	2°18'N	73°17'E	Gemendhoo (U)	Baa	7	5°17'N	73°02'E
Fonimagoodhoo (U)	Baa	7	5°15'N	73°10'E	Gemendhoo (U)	Noonu	5	5°47'N	73°21'E
Foththeyo-bodufushi (U)	Vaavu	13	3°27'N	73°46'E	George Reid (Wk)	Haa Dhaalu	2	6°24'N	72°34'E
Four Seasons Kud Huraa (R)	Kaafu	9	4°19'N	73°36'E	Gesskalhuhera (U)	Seenu	22	0°39'S	73°13'E
Four Seasons Landaa (PR)	Baa	7	5°18'N	73°07'E	Giraavaru (R)	Kaafu	9	4°12'N	73°25'E
Francois (Wk)	Laamu	18	1°53'N	73°14'E	Giraavaru (U)	Raa	6	5°36'N	72°52'E
French Privateer (Wk)	Gaafu Alifu	19	0°46'N	73°08'E	Giraavaru Kuda Haa (P)	Kaafu	9	4°13'N	73°25'E
French Wreck (Wk)	Alifu Alifu	11	4°25'N	72°55'E	Girifushi (U)	Kaafu	9	4°19'N	73°35'E
Fuggiri (U)	Raa	6	5°43'N	72°52'E	Goabilivaadhoo (U)	Noonu	5	5°49'N	73°23'E
Fukumaru (Wk)	Kaafu	9	4°12'N	73°31'E	Goidhoo (I)	Baa	7	4°53'N	73°00'E
Fulangi (U)	Gaafu Alifu	19	0°41'N	73°12'E	Goidhoo (I)	Shaviyani	4	6°26'N	72°56'E
Fulhadhoo (I)	Baa	7	4°53'N	72°56'E	Golhaallaa (U)	Gaafu Dhaalu	20	0°19'N	73°29'E
Fulidhoo (I)	Vaavu	13	3°41'N	73°25'E	Gongalu Huraa (U)	Meemu	16	2°53'N	73°34'E
Full Moon Beach Resort (R)	Kaafu	9	4°15'N	73°33'E	Gosi (U)	Gaafu Dhaalu	20	0°31'N	73°09'E
Fun Island (R)	Kaafu	10	3°52'N	73°28'E	Govvaafushi (U)	Haa Alifu	1	7°01'N	72°55'E
Funadhoo (U)	Baa	7	5°17'N	73°03'E	Govvaafushi (U)	Lhaviyani	8	5°22'N	73°39'E
Funadhoo (U)	Gaafu Alifu	19	0°34'N	73°32'E	Goyyafaru (U)	Raa	6	5°34'N	72°56'E
Funadhoo (U)	Kaafu	9	4°11'N	73°31'E	Guboshi (U)	Raa	6	5°33'N	72°53'E
Funadhoo (R)	Shaviyani	4	6°08'N	73°17'E	Gulhi (I)	Kaafu	10	3°59'N	73°31'E
Funadhooviligili (U)	Gaafu Alifu	19	0°34'N	73°31'E	Gulhi Falhu (P)	Kaafu	9	4°11'N	73°28'E
Funamadhua (PR)	Gaafu Alifu	19	0°31'N	73°13'E	Gulhiggaathuhuraa (U)	Kaafu	10	3°58'N	73°31'E
Fukumaru (Wk)	Kaafu	9	4°12'N	73°31'E	Guraidhoo (I)	Kaafu	10	3°54'N	73°28'E

(PR) - Proposed Resort   (R) - Resort   (U) - Uninhabited Island   (I) - Inhabited Island   (WK) - Wreck   (P) - Protected Marine Area

ISLAND NAME	ATOLL	MAP #	REFERENCE		ISLAND NAME	ATOLL	MAP #	REFERENCE	
Guraidhoo (I)	Thaa	17	2°19'N	73°19'E	Holiday Island (R)	Alifu Dhaalu	12	3°29'N	72°49'E
Guraidhoo (U)	Laamu	18	1°54'N	73°15'E	Hoothodeyaa (U)	Gaafu Dhaalu	20	0°13'N	73°11'E
Guraidhoo Kandu (P)	Kaafu	10	3°54'N	73°28'E	Horubadhoo (U)	Baa	7	5°10'N	73°03'E
Haafushi (U)	Meemu	16	2°47'N	73°26'E	HP Reef (P)	Kaafu	9	4°19'N	73°35'E
Hadahaa (PR)	Gaafu Alifu	19	0°31'N	73°27'E	Hudhufushee Finolhu (U)	Dhaalu	15	2°54'N	72°55'E
Hadoolaafushi (U)	Lhaviyani	8	5°23'N	73°39'E	Hudhufushi (PR)	Lhaviyani	8	5°22'N	73°39'E
Hagedhoo (U)	Gaafu Alifu	19	0°32'N	73°12'E	Huivani (U)	Noonu	5	5°54'N	73°19'E
Hagrandhoo (U)	Gaafu Alifu	19	0°51'N	73°13'E	Hukurudhoo (U)	Alifu Dhaalu	12	3°34'N	72°43'E
Haguvillaa (U)	Gaafu Alifu	19	0°42'N	73°16'E	Hulhedhdhoo (U)	Gaafu Dhaalu	20	0°25'N	73°00'E
Hakuraa Club (R)	Meemu	16	2°51'N	73°32'E	Hulhidhoo (U)	Vaavu	13	3°29'N	73°32'E
Hakura Thila (P)	Meemu	16	2°57'N	73°32'E	Hulhimendhoo (U)	Gaafu Alifu	19	0°43'N	73°26'E
Hakuraahuraa (U)	Meemu	16	2°51'N	73°32'E	Hulhimendhoo (U)	Laamu	18	1°49'N	73°23'E
Halaveli (R)	Alifu Alifu	11	4°02'N	72°56'E	Hulhiyandhoo (U)	Laamu	18	2°05'N	73°33'E
Halaveli Wreck (Wk)	Alifu Alifu	11	4°03'N	72°55'E	Hulhiyanfushi (U)	Thaa	17	2°16'N	73°13'E
Hanghghaameedhoo (I)	Alifu Dhaalu	12	3°51'N	72°58'E	Hulhudhdhoo (U)	Noonu	5	5°49'N	73°19'E
Hanhushi (U)	Laamu	18	1°57'N	73°16'E	Hulhudheli (I)	Dhaalu	15	2°52'N	72°51'E
Hanifaruhuraa (U)	Baa	7	5°11'N	73°09'E	Hulhudhoo (U)	Baa	7	5°04'N	73°02'E
Hanifarurah (U)	Baa	7	5°12'N	73°08'E	Hulhudhoo (U)	Baa	7	5°17'N	73°02'E
Hanimaadhoo (I)	Haa Dhaalu	3	6°45'N	73°10'E	Hulhudhoo (U)	Raa	6	5°44'N	73°01'E
Hankede (PR)	Seenu	22	0°39'S	73°06'E	Hulhudhuffaaru (I)	Raa	6	5°46'N	73°01'E
Hankedehajara (U)	Seenu	22	0°39'S	73°07'E	Hulhule (U)	Kaafu	9	4°12'N	73°32'E
Hans Hass Place (P)	Kaafu	9	4°11'N	73°28'E	Hulhudhoo (I)	Seenu	22	0°36'S	73°14'E
Hathifushi (I)	Haa Alifu	1	7°02'N	72°50'E	Hulhumalé (U)	Kaafu	A	4°13'N	73°32'E
Hathifushi (U)	Thaa	17	2°17'N	73°16'E	Hulhuvehi (U)	Dhaalu	15	2°52'N	73°02'E
Havoddaa (U)	Gaafu Dhaalu	20	0°33'N	73°06'E	Hunigondirehaa (U)	Gaafu Dhaalu	20	0°26'N	73°00'E
Havodigalaa (U)	Gaafu Dhaalu	20	0°32'N	73°05'E	Huraa (I)	Kaafu	9	4°20'N	73°36'E
Hayston (Wk)	Haa Dhaalu	2	6°24'N	72°34'E	Huraa (U)	Haa Alifu	1	6°52'N	72°57'E
Hebadhoo (I)	Noonu	5	5°58'N	73°24'E	Huraa (U)	Haa Dhaalu	3	6°41'N	73°06'E
Hembadhoo (U)	Kaafu	9	4°29'N	73°24'E	Hurasdhoo (U)	Alifu Dhaalu	12	3°40'N	72°47'E
Hembadhoo (Wk)	Kaafu	9	4°29'N	73°24'E	Hurasfaruhuraa (U)	Shaviyani	4	6°08'N	73°03'E
Hedha (U)	Laamu	18	1°50'N	73°17'E	Hurasveli (U)	Meemu	16	3°01'N	73°37'E
Heenfaru (U)	Alifu Dhaalu	12	3°49'N	72°50'E	Huravalhi (U)	Lhaviyani	8	5°31'N	73°27'E
Helengeli (R)	Kaafu	9	4°38'N	73°34'E	Huruelhi (U)	Alifu Dhaalu	12	3°33'N	72°43'E
Heretere (PR)	Seenu	22	0°38'S	73°14'E	Huruvalhi (U)	Raa	6	5°24'N	72°58'E
Hevaahulhudhoo (U)	Gaafu Dhaalu	20	0°18'N	73°02'E	Huthisdhoo (U)	Laamu	18	1°47'N	73°23'E
Hibalhidhoo (U)	Baa	7	5°08'N	73°07'E	Huvadhumaa Vattaru (U)	Noonu	5	5°51'N	73°27'E
Hikahera (U)	Seenu	22	0°35'S	73°14'E	Huvafen Fushi (R)	Kaafu	9	4°22'N	73°22'E
Hilton Maldives (R)	Alifu Dhaalu	12	3°37'N	72°43'E	Huvahandhoo (U)	Haa Alifu	1	6°57'N	72°54'E
Himendhoo (I)	Alifu Alifu	11	3°55'N	72°45'E	Huvahendhoo (U)	Alifu Dhaalu	12	3°39'N	72°58'E
Himithi (U)	Faafu	14	3°16'N	72°49'E	Huvarafushi (I)	Haa Alifu	1	6°58'N	72°53'E
Himmafushi (I)	Kaafu	9	4°19'N	73°34'E	Idimaa (U)	Gaafu Alifu	19	0°24'N	73°34'E
Hinaamaagalaa (U)	Gaafu Alifu	19	0°38'N	73°21'E	Ifuru (U)	Raa	6	5°43'N	73°02'E
Hingaahuraa (U)	Vaavu	13	3°22'N	73°35'E	Iguraidhoo (I)	Raa	6	5°28'N	73°02'E
Hinnavaru (I)	Lhaviyani	8	5°29'N	73°25'E	Iguraidhoo (U)	Noonu	5	5°48'N	73°21'E
Hiraveri (U)	Raa	6	5°34'N	72°52'E	Ihavandhoo (I)	Haa Alifu	1	6°57'N	72°56'E
Hirifushi (U)	Gaafu Alifu	19	0°33'N	73°21'E	Ihuru (U)	Kaafu	9	4°18'N	73°25'E
Hirilandhoo (I)	Thaa	17	2°16'N	72°56'E	Innafinolhu (U)	Haa Alifu	1	7°04'N	72°49'E
Hirimaradhoo (I)	Haa Dhaalu	3	6°43'N	73°01'E	Innafinolhu Wreck (WK)	Haa Alifu	1	7°04'N	72°49'E
Hirinaidhoo (U)	Haa Dhaalu	3	6°42'N	72°57'E	Innafushi (U)	Alifu Dhaalu	12	3°48'N	72°44'E
Hiriyaadhoo (U)	Lhaviyani	8	5°25'N	73°38'E	Innafushi (U)	Baa	7	4°53'N	72°53'E
Hiriyafushi (U)	Dhaalu	15	2°43'N	72°59'E	Innafushi (U)	Haa Dhaalu	2	6°24'N	72°38'E
Hiriyanfushi (U)	Thaa	17	2°13'N	73°09'E	Innamaadhoo (I)	Raa	6	5°33'N	73°03'E
Hirubadhoo (U)	Shaviyani	4	6°12'N	73°15'E	Innarehaa (U)	Gaafu Alifu	19	0°23'N	73°33'E
Hirundhoo (U)	Baa	7	5°13'N	73°09'E	Isdhoo (I)	Laamu	18	2°07'N	73°34'E
Hitaadhoo (I)	Baa	7	5°01'N	72°56'E	Island Hideaway (R)	Haa Alifu	1	6°51'N	73°04'E
Hithaadhoo (U)	Gaafu Alifu	19	0°51'N	73°15'E	Issari (U)	Dhaalu	15	2°43'N	72°59'E
Hithadhoo (I)	Laamu	18	1°48'N	73°23'E	Jinnathugau (U)	Faafu	14	3°12'N	73°00'E
Hithadhoo (I)	Seenu	22	0°37'S	73°05'E	Kaaddoo (U)	Thaa	17	2°17'N	73°15'E
Hiyafushi (U)	Alifu Dhaalu	12	3°28'N	72°53'E	Kaadedhdhoo (U)	Gaafu Dhaalu	20	0°29'N	73°00'E
Hoadedhdhoo (I)	Gaafu Dhaalu	20	0°27'N	73°00'E	Kaalhahuttaa (U)	Gaafu Dhaalu	20	0°14'N	73°08'E
Hodaafushi (PR)	Haa Dhaalu	3	6°47'N	73°07'E	Kaalhehuttaa (U)	Gaafu Dhaalu	20	0°11'N	73°13'E
Hodaidhoo (U)	Haa Dhaalu	3	6°47'N	73°05'E	Kaashidhoo (I)	Kaafu	9	4°57'N	73°28'E
Hodelifushi (U)	Thaa	17	2°30'N	73°19'E	Kaashidhoo (PR)	Gaafu Dhaalu	20	0°20'N	73°26'E
Holhudhoo (I)	Noonu	5	5°46'N	73°16'E	Kaashihulhudhoo (U)	Gaafu Dhaalu	20	0°24'N	73°00'E
Holhumeedhoo (U)	Noonu	5	5°45'N	73°15'E	Kabaalifaru (PR)	Shaviyani	4	6°07'N	73°15'E
Holhurahaa (U)	Laamu	18	2°03'N	73°32'E	Kadahalagalaa (U)	Gaafu Dhaalu	20	0°14'N	73°13'E

(PR) - Proposed Resort   (R) - Resort   (U) - Uninhabited Island   (I) - Inhabited Island   (WK) - Wreck   (P) - Protected Marine Area

ISLAND NAME	ATOLL	MAP #	REFERENCE		ISLAND NAME	ATOLL	MAP #	REFERENCE	
Kadevaarehaa (U)	Gaafu Dhaalu	20	0°26'N	73°00'E	Kelaa (Wk)	Haa Alifu	1	6°57'N	73°13'E
Kadhdhoo (U)	Laamu	18	1°51'N	73°32'E	Kendheraa (U)	Gaafu Alifu	19	0°44'N	73°17'E
Kadimma (U)	Dhaalu	15	2°44'N	73°01'E	Kendhoo (I)	Baa	7	5°17'N	73°01'E
Kadimmahuraa (U)	Noonu	5	5°52'N	73°29'E	Keredhdhoo (U)	Gaafu Dhaalu	20	0°16'N	73°06'E
Kadoodhoo (I)	Thaa	17	2°19'N	72°55'E	Keremitta (U)	Gaafu Dhaalu	20	0°24'N	73°01'E
Kadoo (Wk)	Thaa	17	2°29'N	72°55'E	Keyhuvadhoo (U)	Gaafu Dhaalu	20	0°20'N	73°02'E
Kadoogadu (U)	Raa	6	5°47'N	72°53'E	Keylakuna (U)	Haa Dhaalu	3	6°36'N	73°01'E
Kadufushi (U)	Thaa	17	2°32'N	72°59'E	Keyodhoo (I)	Vaavu	13	3°28'N	73°33'E
Kaduhulhudhoo (I)	Gaafu Alifu	19	0°21'N	73°33'E	Keyodhoo (U)	Baa	7	5°17'N	72°59'E
Kadumoonufushi (U)	Faafu	14	3°18'N	72°54'E	Kibidhoo (I)	Thaa	17	2°10'N	73°04'E
Kaduviligili (U)	Gaafu Alifu	19	0°52'N	73°12'E	Kihaadhoo (I)	Baa	7	5°13'N	73°08'E
Kafathalhaahera (U)	Seenu	22	0°41'S	73°07'E	Kihaadhuffaru (R)	Baa	7	5°12'N	73°08'E
Kafenaa (U)	Gaafu Dhaalu	20	0°32'N	73°00'E	Kihavahhuruvalhi (U)	Baa	7	5°18'N	73°03'E
Kafidhoo (U)	Thaa	17	2°19'N	72°58'E	Kilisfaruhuraa (U)	Shaviyani	4	6°06'N	73°03'E
Kagi (U)	Kaafu	9	4°41'N	73°30'E	Kinolhas (I)	Raa	6	5°27'N	73°02'E
Kaiaidhoo (U)	Noonu	5	5°59'N	73°19'E	Kiraidhoo (U)	Dhaalu	15	2°47'N	73°02'E
Kakai-ariyadhoo (U)	Haa Dhaalu	3	6°28'N	72°54'E	Kisserehaa (U)	Gaafu Alifu	19	0°39'N	73°08'E
Kakolhas (I)	Thaa	17	2°19'N	72°57'E	Koalaa (U)	Noonu	5	5°51'N	73°29'E
Kalhahadhihuraa (U)	Alifu Dhaalu	12	3°48'N	72°43'E	Kodaanafuttaa (U)	Gaafu Dhaalu	20	0°20'N	73°30'E
Kalhaidhoo (I)	Laamu	18	1°59'N	73°32'E	Kodedhoo (U)	Gaafu Dhaalu	20	0°25'N	73°00'E
Kalhefalaa (U)	Gaafu Dhaalu	20	0°21'N	73°02'E	Kodegalaa (U)	Gaafu Dhaalu	20	0°23'N	73°24'E
Kalhehigili (U)	Gaafu Dhaalu	20	0°18'N	73°02'E	Kodey (I)	Gaafu Alifu	19	0°30'N	73°33'E
Kalherehaa (U)	Gaafu Dhaalu	20	0°15'N	73°20'E	Kodeymatheelaabadhoo (U)	Gaafu Alifu	19	0°31'N	73°30'E
Kalhudheyfushi (U)	Thaa	17	2°18'N	73°17'E	Kodeyviligili (U)	Gaafu Alifu	19	0°31'N	73°33'E
Kalhufahalafushi (PR)	Thaa	17	2°25'N	73°22'E	Kodghutigalla (U)	Gaafu Dhaalu	20	0°17'N	73°12'E
Kalhuhuraa (U)	Kaafu	10	4°01'N	73°22'E	Kodufuttaa (U)	Gaafu Alifu	19	0°41'N	73°26'E
Kalhuhuttaa (U)	Gaafu Dhaalu	20	0°20'N	73°02'E	Kodurataa (U)	Gaafu Dhaalu	20	0°23'N	73°02'E
Kalhumanjehuraa (U)	Lhaviyani	8	5°33'N	73°30'E	Kolaa (U)	Gaafu Alifu	19	0°50'N	73°11'E
Kalhuoiyfinolhu (U)	Lhaviyani	8	5°22'N	73°38'E	Kolamaafushi (I)	Gaafu Alifu	19	0°50'N	73°11'E
Kalhuohfummi (Wk)	Meemu	16	2°47'N	73°26'E	Kolhufushi (U)	Noonu	5	5°48'N	73°28'E
Kalhurahaa (U)	Laamu	18	1°51'N	73°16'E	Kolhufushi (U)	Thaa	17	2°16'N	73°13'E
Kaludirehaa (U)	Gaafu Alifu	19	0°26'N	73°34'E	Kolhufushi (U)	Thaa	17	2°22'N	73°22'E
Kamadhoo (I)	Baa	7	5°17'N	73°08'E	Kolhufushi (I)	Meemu	16	2°46'N	73°26'E
Kanamana (U)	Haa Dhaalu	3	6°43'N	72°54'E	Komandhoo (I)	Shaviyani	4	6°03'N	73°04'E
Kanandhoo (U)	Gaafu Dhaalu	20	0°16'N	73°04'E	Komandhoo (R)	Lhaviyani	8	5°29'N	73°26'E
Kandaru (U)	Laamu	18	2°03'N	73°32'E	Konottaa (PR)	Gaafu Dhaalu	20	0°28'N	73°09'E
Kandaru (U)	Thaa	17	2°19'N	73°19'E	Kooddoo (U)	Gaafu Alifu	19	0°44'N	73°26'E
Kandhja Ali Madath (Wk)	Kaafu	A	4°11'N	73°31'E	Kothaifaru (U)	Raa	6	5°32'N	72°51'E
Kandholhudhoo (I)	Raa	6	5°37'N	72°52'E	Kottafaru (U)	Raa	6	5°31'N	72°52'E
Kandholhudhoo (U)	Alifu Alifu	11	4°00'N	72°53'E	Kottefaru (U)	Raa	6	5°31'N	73°03'E
Kanditeem (I)	Shaviyani	4	6°26'N	72°55'E	Kuburudhoo (I)	Haa Dhaalu	3	6°39'N	73°02'E
Kandooma (R)	Kaafu	10	3°54'N	73°28'E	Kuda Anbaraa (U)	Vaavu	13	3°26'N	73°26'E
Kandoomafushi (U)	Kaafu	10	3°54'N	73°28'E	Kuda Giri (Wk)	Kaafu	10	3°58'N	73°30'E
Kandu Huraa (U)	Seenu	22	0°37'S	73°09'E	Kuda Huraa (U)	Kaafu	9	4°19'N	73°36'E
Kanduoiygiri (U)	Kaafu	9	4°16'N	73°32'E	Kuda Kandiheraganda (U)	Seenu	22	0°37'S	73°08'E
Kani (U)	Thaa	17	2°12'N	72°58'E	Kuda Wataru (U)	Kaafu	9	4°16'N	73°23'E
Kanifinolhu (U)	Kaafu	9	4°21'N	73°36'E	Kudabados (U)	Kaafu	9	4°16'N	73°30'E
Kanifushi (U)	Baa	7	5°01'N	72°57'E	Kudadhoo (U)	Alifu Dhaalu	12	3°28'N	72°53'E
Kanifushi (PR)	Lhaviyani	8	5°22'N	73°20'E	Kudadhoo (U)	Baa	7	5°02'N	72°59'E
Kanimeedhoo (U)	Thaa	17	2°12'N	73°07'E	Kudadhoo (U)	Lhaviyani	8	5°30'N	73°27'E
Kanneiyfaru (U)	Dhaalu	15	2°56'N	73°02'E	Kudadhoo (U)	Shaviyani	4	6°26'N	72°54'E
Kannigallaa (U)	Gaafu Dhaalu	20	0°27'N	73°00'E	Kudadhoo (U)	Thaa	17	2°18'N	72°57'E
Kanuoui Huraa (U)	Kaafu	9	4°19'N	73°36'E	Kudafaress (U)	Laamu	18	1°48'N	73°18'E
Kanuhuraa (R)	Lhaviyani	8	5°32'N	73°31'E	Kudafari (I)	Noonu	5	5°53'N	73°24'E
Kaohera (U)	Seenu	22	0°36'S	73°06'E	Kudafarufasgandu (U)	Haa Dhaalu	3	6°43'N	72°56'E
Karibeyru Thila (P)	Alifu Alifu	11	4°06'N	72°57'E	Kudafehela (U)	Gaafu Alifu	19	0°26'N	73°34'E
Karimma (U)	Noonu	5	5°39'N	73°23'E	Kudafinolhu (U)	Haa Alifu	1	6°59'N	72°53'E
Kashidhoo (U)	Baa	7	5°18'N	72°58'E	Kudafinolhu (U)	Kaafu	10	3°52'N	73°28'E
Kattalafushi (U)	Haa Dhaalu	3	6°34'N	72°59'E	Kudafolhudhoo (U)	Alifu Alifu	11	4°11'N	72°46'E
Kedevaahera (U)	Seenu	22	0°34'S	73°13'E	Kudafunafaru (PR)	Noonu	5	5°53'N	73°23'E
Kedhigadu (U)	Dhaalu	15	2°42'N	72°51'E	Kudafushi (U)	Laamu	18	1°47'N	73°19'E
Kedhikulhudhoo (I)	Noonu	5	5°57'N	73°25'E	Kudafushi (U)	Noonu	5	5°43'N	73°25'E
Kedhivaru (U)	Noonu	5	5°51'N	73°20'E	Kudafushi (U)	Raa	6	5°31'N	72°59'E
Keekimini (U)	Shaviyani	4	6°01'N	73°07'E	Kudafuttaa (U)	Gaafu Alifu	19	0°48'N	73°13'E
Kekuraalhuveli (U)	Meemu	16	2°51'N	73°32'E	Kudahaiykodi (U)	Raa	6	5°36'N	72°59'E
Kelaa (I)	Haa Alifu	1	6°57'N	73°13'E	Kudahithi (R)	Kaafu	9	4°25'N	73°23'E

(PR) - Proposed Resort　　(R) - Resort　　(U) - Uninhabited Island　　(I) - Inhabited Island　　(WK) - Wreck　　(P) - Protected Marine Area

ISLAND NAME	ATOLL	MAP #	REFERENCE
Kudahuraa (U)	Laamu	18	1°51'N 73°32'E
Kudahuvadhoo (I)	Dhaalu	15	2°40'N 72°54'E
Kudakaaddoo (U)	Thaa	17	2°17'N 73°16'E
Kudakalhaidhoo (U)	Laamu	18	1°59'N 73°32'E
Kudakibidhoo (U)	Thaa	17	2°10'N 73°04'E
Kudakurathu (U)	Raa	6	5°35'N 73°03'E
Kudalafari (U)	Gaafu Alifu	19	0°54'N 73°21'E
Kudalhaimendhoo (U)	Shaviyani	4	6°01'N 73°18'E
Kudalhosgiri (U)	Raa	6	5°36'N 72°55'E
Kudamuraidhoo (PR)	Haa Dhaalu	3	6°38'N 72°55'E
Kudanaagoashi (U)	Haa Dhaalu	3	6°41'N 72°54'E
Kudarah (R)	Alifu Dhaalu	12	3°34'N 72°55'E
Kudarah Thila (P)	Alifu Dhaalu	12	3°34'N 72°55'E
Kudarikilu (I)	Baa	7	5°18'N 73°04'E
Kudathulhaadhoo (U)	Raa	6	5°24'N 72°54'E
Kudausfushi (PR)	Meemu	16	2°49'N 73°27'E
Kuddrah (U)	Noonu	5	5°50'N 73°19'E
Kudhebondeyyaa (U)	Gaafu Alifu	19	0°25'N 73°35'E
Kudhehulhedhdhoo (U)	Gaafu Dhaalu	20	0°27'N 73°00'E
Kudhekelaihuttaa (U)	Gaafu Dhaalu	20	0°13'N 73°11'E
Kudhelifadhoo (U)	Gaafu Dhaalu	20	0°24'N 73°01'E
Kudhiboli (U)	Vaavu	13	3°38'N 73°22'E
Kudi Maa (Wk)	Alifu Dhaalu	12	3°36'N 72°53'E
Kukulhudhoo (U)	Raa	6	5°28'N 72°52'E
Kukurahaa (U)	Laamu	18	1°52'N 73°16'E
Kulhuduffushi (I)	Haa Dhaalu	3	6°37'N 73°04'E
Kumundhoo (I)	Haa Dhaalu	3	6°34'N 73°03'E
Kunahandhoo (I)	Laamu	18	1°47'N 73°22'E
Kunavashi (U)	Vaavu	13	3°37'N 73°23'E
Kunburudhoo (I)	Alifu Dhaalu	12	3°47'N 72°56'E
Kunfunadhoo (U)	Baa	7	5°07'N 73°04'E
Kunnamaloa (U)	Noonu	5	5°55'N 73°09'E
Kuradhigandu (U)	Meemu	16	2°46'N 73°23'E
Kurali (U)	Meemu	16	2°47'N 73°22'E
Kuramaadhoo (U)	Noonu	5	5°53'N 73°08'E
Kuramathi (R)	Alifu Alifu	11	4°16'N 72°59'E
Kurandhuvaru (U)	Thaa	17	2°33'N 73°11'E
Kuredhdhoo (U)	Lhaviyani	8	5°33'N 73°28'E
Kuredhdhoo (U)	Gaafu Alifu	19	0°39'N 73°26'E
Kuredhifushi (U)	Thaa	17	2°10'N 73°02'E
Kuredhigadu (U)	Kaafu	9	4°15'N 73°33'E
Kuredhivaru (U)	Noonu	5	5°53'N 73°21'E
Kuredu (R)	Lhaviyani	8	5°33'N 73°28'E
Kuredu Express (P)	Lhaviyani	8	5°33'N 73°29'E
Kurendhoo (I)	Lhaviyani	8	5°20'N 73°28'E
Kuribi (I)	Haa Dhaalu	3	6°40'N 72°59'E
Kuroshigiri (U)	Raa	6	5°31'N 72°53'E
Kurumba Village (R)	Kaafu	9	4°13'N 73°31'E
Lady Christine (Wk)	Kaafu	9	4°46'N 73°23'E
Laguna Maldives (R)	Kaafu	10	4°07'N 73°26'E
Laihaa (U)	Gaafu Dhaalu	20	0°15'N 73°20'E
Landaa Giraavaru (R)	Baa	7	5°18'N 73°07'E
Landhoo (I)	Noonu	5	5°53'N 73°28'E
Langon Bank (Wk)	Laamu	18	2°06'N 73°31'E
Lankanfinolhu (U)	Kaafu	9	4°17'N 73°33'E
Lankanfushi (U)	Kaafu	9	4°18'N 73°33'E
Lankan Thila (P)	Kaafu	9	4°17'N 73°32'E
Lhaabugali (U)	Raa	6	5°33'N 72°53'E
Lhaimagu (I)	Shaviyani	4	6°10'N 73°15'E
Lhanbugau (U)	Raa	6	5°44'N 72°55'E
Lhavaddoo (U)	Thaa	17	2°18'N 73°18'E
Lhazikuraadi (P)	Meemu	16	2°57'N 73°32'E
Lhohi (I)	Noonu	5	5°49'N 73°23'E
Lhohi (U)	Dhaalu	15	2°57'N 72°59'E
Lhohi (U)	Lhaviyani	8	5°19'N 73°28'E
Lhohi (U)	Raa	6	5°28'N 72°53'E
Lhohifushi (R)	Kaafu	9	4°21'N 73°37'E
Lhosfushi (U)	Kaafu	10	3°54'N 73°28'E
Lhossaa (U)	Gaafu Alifu	19	0°49'N 73°12'E
Lhossalafushi (U)	Lhaviyani	8	5°19'N 73°29'E
Liboakandhoo (U)	Raa	6	5°44'N 72°56'E
Lily Beach (R)	Alifu Dhaalu	12	3°39'N 72°58'E
Lions Head (P)	Kaafu	9	4°11'N 73°26'E
Loafaru (U)	Noonu	5	5°47'N 73°17'E
Lonudhoo (U)	Gaafu Dhaalu	20	0°19'N 73°25'E
Lonudhoohuttaa (PR)	Gaafu Dhaalu	20	0°18'N 73°25'E
Lundhufushi (PR)	Raa	6	5°38'N 72°59'E
Maabaidhoo (I)	Laamu	18	2°02'N 73°32'E
Maabinhuraa (U)	Lhaviyani	8	5°21'N 73°39'E
Maaddoo (U)	Baa	7	5°06'N 73°04'E
Maadheli (U)	Dhaalu	15	2°53'N 72°50'E
Maadhiguvaru (U)	Gaafu Alifu	19	0°42'N 73°16'E
Maadhoo (U)	Kaafu	10	3°52'N 73°28'E
Maaeboodhoo (I)	Dhaalu	15	2°42'N 72°58'E
Maaehivakaa (U)	Gaafu Dhaalu	20	0°17'N 73°03'E
Maafahi (I)	Haa Alifu	1	6°50'N 73°09'E
Maafaru (I)	Noonu	5	5°49'N 73°29'E
Maafaru (U)	Raa	6	5°27'N 72°54'E
Maafehelaa (U)	Gaafu Alifu	19	0°23'N 73°33'E
Maafilaafushi (U)	Lhaviyani	8	5°22'N 73°25'E
Maafinolhu (U)	Haa Alifu	1	7°00'N 72°52'E
Maafunafaru (U)	Noonu	5	5°52'N 73°22'E
Maafushi (I)	Kaafu	10	3°57'N 73°29'E
Maafushi (U)	Dhaalu	15	2°42'N 72°52'E
Maafushi (U)	Faafu	14	3°15'N 72°59'E
Maafushivaru (U)	Alifu Dhaalu	12	3°37'N 72°54'E
Maagaa (U)	Alifu Alifu	11	3°59'N 72°58'E
Maagalaa (U)	Gaafu Dhaalu	20	0°23'N 73°23'E
Maagau (U)	Dhaalu	15	2°57'N 72°55'E
Maagefuttaa (U)	Gaafu Alifu	19	0°51'N 73°11'E
Maagodirehaa (U)	Gaafu Dhaalu	20	0°31'N 73°00'E
Maagulhi (U)	Thaa	17	2°32'N 73°11'E
Maahera (U)	Seenu	22	0°36'S 73°06'E
Maahuraa (U)	Meemu	16	2°48'N 73°26'E
Maakandoodhoo (I)	Shaviyani	4	6°14'N 73°16'E
Maakalhuveli (U)	Laamu	18	1°47'N 73°20'E
Maakanaarataa (U)	Gaafu Alifu	19	0°49'N 73°12'E
Maakurandhoo (U)	Noonu	5	5°42'N 73°18'E
Maakurathu (I)	Raa	6	5°37'N 73°03'E
Maalefaru (U)	Dhaalu	15	2°53'N 73°02'E
Maalefushi (PR)	Thaa	17	2°18'N 73°18'E
Maalhaveli (U)	Meemu	16	2°54'N 73°35'E
Maalhendhoo (I)	Noonu	5	5°54'N 73°27'E
Maalhoss (I)	Alifu Alifu	11	3°59'N 72°43'E
Maalhoss (I)	Baa	7	5°08'N 73°07'E
Maamaduvvari (U)	Baa	7	5°01'N 72°56'E
Maamendhoo (I)	Gaafu Alifu	19	0°43'N 73°26'E
Maamendhoo (I)	Laamu	18	1°49'N 73°23'E
Maamigili (I)	Alifu Dhaalu	12	3°28'N 72°50'E
Maamigili (U)	Raa	6	5°39'N 72°53'E
Maamunagau (U)	Raa	6	5°22'N 72°55'E
Maamunagaufinolhu (U)	Raa	6	5°23'N 72°52'E
Maamutaa (U)	Gaafu Alifu	19	0°51'N 73°25'E
Maanaagalaa (U)	Gaafu Alifu	19	0°53'N 73°20'E
Maandhoo (U)	Laamu	18	1°52'N 73°32'E
Maanenfushi (PR)	Raa	6	5°45'N 72°58'E
Maarandhoo (I)	Haa Alifu	1	6°52'N 72°59'E
Maarehaa (U)	Gaafu Alifu	19	0°28'N 73°34'E
Maarikilu (U)	Baa	7	5°20'N 72°57'E
Maashigiri (U)	Raa	6	5°31'N 72°49'E
Maathoda (I)	Gaafu Dhaalu	20	0°12'N 73°11'E
Maaugoodhoo (I)	Shaviyani	4	6°02'N 73°17'E

(PR) - Proposed Resort   (R) - Resort   (U) - Uninhabited Island   (I) - Inhabited Island   (WK) - Wreck   (P) - Protected Marine Area

ISLAND NAME	ATOLL	MAP #	REFERENCE	
Maausfushi (U)	Meemu	16	2°48'N	73°26'E
Maavaafushi (U)	Lhaviyani	8	5°22'N	73°22'E
Maavaarulaa (U)	Gaafu Dhaalu	20	0°21'N	73°31'E
Maavah (I)	Laamu	18	1°53'N	73°14'E
Maavaidhoo (I)	Haa Dhaalu	3	6°31'N	73°03'E
Maavaruhuraa (U)	Faafu	14	3°11'N	73°03'E
Maaveahi (U)	Laamu	18	1°50'N	73°17'E
Maavedhdhoo (U)	Gaafu Dhaalu	20	0°18'N	73°29'E
Maavelavaru (PR)	Noonu	5	5°48'N	73°10'E
Maaya Thila (P)	Alifu Alifu	11	4°05'N	72°52'E
Maayafushi (R)	Alifu Alifu	11	4°04'N	72°53'E
Machchafushi (R)	Alifu Dhaalu	12	3°36'N	72°53'E
Madaveli (I)	Gaafu Dhaalu	20	0°28'N	73°00'E
Madhiriguraidhoo (R)	Lhaviyani	8	5°28'N	73°34'E
Madhirivaadhoo (U)	Baa	7	5°16'N	73°09'E
Madidhoo (U)	Shaviyani	4	6°18'N	73°07'E
Madifushi (I)	Meemu	16	3°05'N	73°38'E
Madifushi (I)	Thaa	17	2°22'N	73°21'E
Madihera (U)	Seenu	22	0°42'S	73°11'E
Madikuredhdhoo (U)	Shaviyani	4	6°17'N	73°09'E
Madivaafaru (U)	Raa	6	5°37'N	72°58'E
Madivaru (U)	Kaafu	9	4°30'N	73°22'E
Madivaru (U)	Lhaviyani	8	5°28'N	73°22'E
Madivaru (U)	Alifu Alifu	11	4°16'N	73°01'E
Madivaru (P)	Alifu Dhaalu	12	3°36'N	72°43'E
Madivaru Finolhu (U)	Alifu Alifu	11	4°17'N	73°01'E
Madivaruhuraa (U)	Faafu	14	3°16'N	73°01'E
Madi-Ge (Wk)	Alifu Dhaalu	12	3°37'N	72°47'E
Madoogali (R)	Alifu Alifu	11	4°06'N	72°45'E
Madulu (U)	Haa Alifu	1	7°03'N	72°57'E
Maduvvari (I)	Meemu	16	3°07'N	73°34'E
Maduvvari (I)	Raa	6	5°29'N	72°54'E
Maduvvari (U)	Lhaviyani	8	5°17'N	73°30'E
Magoodhoo (I)	Faafu	14	3°05'N	72°58'E
Magoodhoo (I)	Noonu	5	5°47'N	73°22'E
Magoodhoofinolhu (U)	Faafu	14	3°04'N	72°57'E
Magudhdhuvaa (U)	Gaafu Dhaalu	20	0°17'N	73°21'E
Mahaana Elhi Huraa (U)	Kaafu	10	3°49'N	73°24'E
Mahadhdhoo (PR)	Gaafu Alifu	19	0°35'N	73°31'E
Mahakanfushi (U)	Laamu	18	1°58'N	73°33'E
Mahibadhoo (I)	Alifu Dhaalu	12	3°45'N	72°58'E
Mahidhoo (U)	Raa	6	5°34'N	72°57'E
Mahutigalla (U)	Gaafu Dhaalu	20	0°16'N	73°12'E
Maidhoo (U)	Lhaviyani	8	5°24'N	73°39'E
Makunudhoo (I)	Haa Dhaalu	2	6°24'N	72°42'E
Makunudhoo Wreck (WK)	Haa Dhaalu	2	6°24'N	72°42'E
Makunudhoo (U)	Kaafu	9	4°32'N	73°24'E
Makunudhoo Kandu (P)	Kaafu	9	4°34'N	73°23'E
Makunudu (R)	Kaafu	9	4°32'N	73°24'E
Makunueri (U)	Faafu	14	3°16'N	72°56'E
Makunufushi (U)	Kaafu	10	3°55'N	73°28'E
Maldives Hilton (R)	Alifu Dhaalu	12	3°37'N	72°44'E
Maldives Victory (Wk)	Kaafu	9	4°11'N	73°31'E
Malé (I)	Kaafu	9	4°11'N	73°31'E
Mallaarehaa (U)	Gaafu Dhaalu	20	0°30'N	73°00'E
Manadhoo (I)	Noonu	5	5°46'N	73°25'E
Manafaru (PR)	Haa Alifu	1	7°00'N	72°57'E
Mandhoo (I)	Alifu Dhaalu	12	3°42'N	72°43'E
Maniyafushi (U)	Kaafu	10	4°03'N	73°24'E
Maradhoo (I)	Seenu	22	0°40'S	73°07'E
Maradhoo-Feydhoo (I)	Seenu	22	0°40'S	73°07'E
Mariyamkoyyerataa (U)	Gaafu Dhaalu	20	0°18'N	73°29'E
Maroshi (I)	Shaviyani	4	6°13'N	73°04'E
Mathaidhoo (U)	Gaafu Dhaalu	20	0°19'N	73°02'E
Matheerah (U)	Haa Alifu	1	7°02'N	72°49'E
Mattidhoo (U)	Gaafu Alifu	19	0°40'N	73°23'E
Mathidhoo (U)	Thaa	17	2°21'N	73°21'E
Mathihuttaa (U)	Gaafu Dhaalu	20	0°16'N	73°21'E
Mathikeranahuttaa (U)	Gaafu Dhaalu	20	0°24'N	73°00'E
Mathikomandoo (U)	Shaviyani	4	6°04'N	73°03'E
Mathivereefinolhu (U)	Alifu Alifu	11	4°11'N	72°45'E
Mathiveri (I)	Alifu Alifu	11	4°12'N	72°44'E
Maththureha (U)	Gaafu Alifu	19	0°22'N	73°33'E
Matu (U)	Gaafu Alifu	19	0°53'N	73°20'E
Mayyaafushi (U)	Lhaviyani	8	5°21'N	73°39'E
Medhadihuraa (U)	Lhaviyani	8	5°33'N	73°31'E
Medhafushi (U)	Haa Alifu	1	7°01'N	72°56'E
Medhafushi (U)	Laamu	18	1°58'N	73°33'E
Medhafushi (U)	Lhaviyani	8	5°22'N	73°26'E
Medhafushi (PR)	Noonu	5	5°44'N	73°19'E
Medhafushi (U)	Thaa	17	2°21'N	73°21'E
Medhuburiyaa (U)	Gaafu Alifu	19	0°23'N	73°33'E
Medhufaru (U)	Noonu	5	5°44'N	73°25'E
Medhufinolhu (U)	Baa	7	5°01'N	72°57'E
Medhufinolhu (R)	Kaafu	9	4°31'N	73°22'E
Medhufinolhu (U)	Laamu	18	2°04'N	73°32'E
Medhufushi (U)	Meemu	16	2°53'N	73°34'E
Medhugiri (U)	Vaavu	13	3°23'N	73°29'E
Medhuhuttaa (U)	Gaafu Alifu	19	0°28'N	73°34'E
Medhukuburudhoo (U)	Shaviyani	4	6°12'N	73°02'E
Medhurah (U)	Shaviyani	4	6°02'N	73°04'E
Medhurehaa (U)	Gaafu Alifu	19	0°22'N	73°33'E
Medhuvinagandu (U)	Laamu	18	1°50'N	73°16'E
Medufinolhu (U)	Alifu Dhaalu	12	3°31'N	72°55'E
Meedhaahuraa (U)	Lhaviyani	8	5°22'N	73°24'E
Meedhoo (I)	Seenu	22	0°36'S	73°14'E
Meedhoo (I)	Dhaalu	15	3°00'N	73°01'E
Meedhoo (I)	Raa	6	5°27'N	72°57'E
Meedhuffushi (U)	Dhaalu	15	3°00'N	73°00'E
Meedhupparu (R)	Raa	6	5°27'N	72°59'E
Meehunthibeyhuttaa (U)	Gaafu Dhaalu	20	0°15'N	73°06'E
Meeru (R)	Kaafu	9	4°28'N	73°43'E
Meerufenfushi (U)	Kaafu	9	4°28'N	73°43'E
Melaimu (U)	Gaafu Alifu	19	0°52'N	73°11'E
Mendhoo (U)	Baa	7	5°11'N	72°59'E
Mendhoo (U)	Laamu	18	1°47'N	73°23'E
Menthandhoo (U)	Gaafu Dhaalu	20	0°20'N	73°30'E
Meradhoo (PR)	Gaafu Alifu	19	0°35'N	73°06'E
Merengihuttaa (U)	Gaafu Dhaalu	20	0°16'N	73°04'E
Mey-yyafushi (U)	Lhaviyani	8	5°27'N	73°36'E
Meyragillaa (U)	Gaafu Dhaalu	20	0°14'N	73°07'E
Migoodhoo (U)	Shaviyani	4	6°14'N	73°14'E
Miladhoo (I)	Noonu	5	5°48'N	73°22'E
Milaidhoo (U)	Baa	7	5°16'N	73°08'E
Milandhoo (U)	Shaviyani	4	6°17'N	73°15'E
Minaavaru (U)	Noonu	5	5°46'N	73°21'E
Minimasgali (U)	Dhaalu	15	2°45'N	72°53'E
Minimasgali (U)	Faafu	14	3°15'N	73°50'E
Minimessaa (U)	Gaafu Alifu	19	0°33'N	73°08'E
Miriyandhoo (U)	Baa	7	5°04'N	73°02'E
Mirihi (R)	Alifu Dhaalu	12	3°37'N	72°47'E
Miyaru Kandu (P)	Vaavu	13	3°35'N	73°30'E
Moofushi (R)	Alifu Dhaalu	12	3°53'N	72°44'E
Mudhdhoo (U)	Baa	7	5°13'N	73°05'E
Mudhimaahuttaa (U)	Gaafu Dhaalu	20	0°16'N	73°21'E
Muiri (U)	Haa Dhaalu	3	6°39'N	72°56'E
Mulhadhoo (I)	Haa Alifu	1	7°01'N	73°00'E
Muli (I)	Meemu	16	2°55'N	73°35'E
Mulidhoo (U)	Haa Alifu	1	6°51'N	73°01'E
Mulikede (PR)	Seenu	22	0°39'S	73°13'E
Mullaafushi (U)	Raa	6	5°32'N	72°54'E
Munandhoo (PR)	Gaafu Alifu	19	0°36'N	73°30'E

(PR) - Proposed Resort   (R) - Resort   (U) - Uninhabited Island   (I) - Inhabited Island   (WK) - Wreck   (P) - Protected Marine Area

ISLAND NAME	ATOLL	MAP #	REFERENCE
Mundoo (I)	Laamu	18	2°01'N 73°32'E
Munnafushi (U)	Laamu	18	1°59'N 73°18'E
Muraidhoo (I)	Haa Alifu	1	6°51'N 73°10'E
Muravandhoo (U)	Raa	6	5°37'N 72°57'E
Mushimasmingili (U)	Alifu Alifu	11	3°57'N 72°55'E
Musleiygihuraa (U)	Lhaviyani	8	5°33'N 73°30'E
Muthaafushi (U)	Baa	7	5°05'N 72°53'E
Naainfarufinolhu (U)	Shaviyani	4	6°12'N 73°00'E
Naalaafushi (I)	Meemu	16	2°53'N 73°34'E
Naamuli Wreck (Wk)	Baa	7	4°51'N 72°51'E
Nadallaa (I)	Gaafu Dhaalu	20	0°18'N 73°02'E
Naibukaloabodufushi (U)	Dhaalu	15	2°46'N 73°02'E
Naifaru (I)	Lhaviyani	8	5°27'N 73°22'E
Naivaadhoo (I)	Haa Dhaalu	3	6°45'N 72°56'E
Nakatchafushi (U)	Kaafu	9	4°22'N 73°22'E
Nalaguraidhoo (U)	Alifu Dhaalu	12	3°29'N 72°48'E
Nalandhoo (U)	Shaviyani	4	6°19'N 73°14'E
Naridhoo (PR)	Haa Alifu	1	6°54'N 73°08'E
Narudhoo (I)	Shaviyani	4	6°16'N 73°13'E
Naruribudhoo (U)	Shaviyani	4	6°17'N 73°12'E
Nassimo Thila (P)	Kaafu	9	4°17'N 73°32'E
Nelivarufinolhu (U)	Baa	7	5°07'N 73°05'E
Nellaidhoo (I)	Haa Dhaalu	3	6°43'N 72°57'E
Neykurendhoo (I)	Haa Dhaalu	3	6°33'N 72°59'E
Neyo (U)	Raa	6	5°29'N 73°03'E
Neyo (U)	Shaviyani	4	6°27'N 73°03'E
Nibiligaa (U)	Baa	7	5°11'N 72°57'E
Nicolaos Embricos (Wk)	Gaafu Alifu	19	0°50'N 73°25'E
Nika (R)	Alifu Alifu	11	4°11'N 72°46'E
Nilandhoo (I)	Faafu	14	3°03'N 72°53'E
Nilandhoo (I)	Gaafu Alifu	19	0°38'N 73°27'E
Nolhivaramu (I)	Haa Dhaalu	3	6°40'N 73°05'E
Nolhivaranfaru (I)	Haa Dhaalu	3	6°42'N 73°07'E
Noomaraa (I)	Shaviyani	4	6°26'N 73°04'E
Oceana (Wk)	Haa Alifu	1	7°07'N 72°53'E
Ocean Reef Club (R)	Seenu	22	0°42'S 73°10'E
Odagallaa (U)	Gaafu Alifu	19	0°40'N 73°25'E
Olhahali (U)	Kaafu	9	4°41'N 73°27'E
Olhimuttaa (U)	Gaafu Dhaalu	20	0°21'N 73°02'E
Olhudhiyafushi (U)	Thaa	17	2°17'N 73°15'E
Olhufushi (U)	Thaa	17	2°22'N 72°54'E
Olhufushi Finolhu (U)	Thaa	17	2°22'N 72°54'E
Olhugiri (U)	Baa	7	5°00'N 72°54'E
Olhugiri (U)	Thaa	17	2°30'N 73°16'E
Olhurataa (U)	Gaafu Dhaalu	20	0°19'N 73°02'E
Olhutholhu (U)	Laamu	18	1°48'N 73°21'E
Olhuveli (R)	Kaafu	10	3°51'N 73°28'E
Olhuveli (U)	Dhaalu	15	2°41'N 72°56'E
Olhuveli (PR)	Laamu	18	1°49'N 73°24'E
Olhuvelifushi (I)	Lhaviyani	8	5°17'N 73°36'E
Oligandufinolhu (U)	Kaafu	10	3°49'N 73°25'E
Omadhoo (I)	Alifu Dhaalu	12	3°47'N 72°58'E
Omadhoo (I)	Thaa	17	2°10'N 73°01'E
One & Only Kanuhura (R)	Lhaviyani	8	5°32'N 73°31'E
One & Only Reethi Rah (R)	Kaafu	9	4°31N 73°22E
Ookolhufinolhu (U)	Lhaviyani	8	5°17'N 73°37'E
Orimas Thila (P)	Alifu Alifu	11	3°59'N 72°57'E
Orimasvaru (U)	Noonu	5	5°52'N 73°12'E
Orivaru (U)	Noonu	5	5°48'N 73°18'E
Palm Beach Resort (R)	Lhaviyani	8	5°28'N 73°34'E
Palm Tree Island (R)	Kaafu	10	3°58'N 73°31'E
Paradise (R)	Kaafu	9	4°17'N 73°33'E
Passenger Liner (Wk)	Gaafu Alifu	19	0°46'N 73°26'E
Pearl Island (R)	Raa	6	5°27'N 72°59'E
Persia Merchant (Wk)	Haa Dhaalu	2	6°24'N 72°34'E
Pioneer (Wk)	Vaavu	13	3°21'N 73°35'E
Prazer E Allegria (Wk)	Meemu	16	2°55'N 73°35'E
Raabandhihuraa (U)	Meemu	16	3°06'N 73°23'E
Raafushi (U)	Noonu	5	5°39'N 73°18'E
Raalhulaakolhu (U)	Noonu	5	5°41'N 73°24'E
Raavehrehaa (U)	Gaafu Alifu	19	0°46'N 73°26'E
Radhdhiggaa (U)	Alifu Dhaalu	12	3°46'N 72°47'E
Raggadu (U)	Vaavu	13	3°25'N 73°23'E
Rahadhoo (U)	Gaafu Dhaalu	20	0°31'N 73°00'E
Raiymandhoo (I)	Meemu	16	3°06'N 73°38'E
Raiyruhhuraa (U)	Lhaviyani	8	5°24'N 73°39'E
Rakeedhoo (I)	Vaavu	13	3°19'N 73°28'E
Ralhe Odagallaa (U)	Gaafu Dhaalu	20	0°19'N 73°23'E
Randheli (PR)	Noonu	5	5°42'N 73°21'E
Rándi 11 (Wk)	Alifu Dhaalu	12	3°30'N 72°54'E
Rangali (U)	Alifu Dhaalu	12	3°37'N 72°43'E
Rangali Finolhu (U)	Alifu Dhaalu	12	3°37'N 72°44'E
Rannalhi (R)	Kaafu	10	3°54'N 73°22'E
Rannamari (Wk)	Kaafu	9	4°18'N 73°25'E
Ranveli (R)	Alifu Dhaalu	12	3°37'N 72°58'E
Rasdhoo (I)	Alifu Alifu	11	4°16'N 73°00'E
Rasfari (P)	Kaafu	9	4°24'N 73°21'E
Rasfari (U)	Kaafu	9	4°24'N 73°21'E
Rasfushi (U)	Haa Dhaalu	3	6°43'N 72°55'E
Rasgetheemu (I)	Raa	6	5°49'N 73°00'E
Rashukolhuhuraa (U)	Alifu Dhaalu	12	3°31'N 72°55'E
Rasmaadhoo (I)	Raa	6	5°34'N 73°03'E
Rathafandhoo (I)	Gaafu Dhaalu	20	0°15'N 73°06'E
Rayvilla Wreck (Wk)	Meemu	16	2°59'N 73°25'E
Redhdhfuttaa (U)	Gaafu Dhaalu	20	0°20'N 73°30'E
Reethi Beach (R)	Baa	7	5°15'N 73°10'E
Reethi Rah (R)	Kaafu	9	4°31'N 73°22'E
Reindeer (Wk)	Alifu Alifu	11	4°15'N 73°00'E
Ravesteyn (Wk)	Alifu Alifu	11	4°16'N 72°44'E
Rhandi 11 (Wk)	Alifu Dhaalu	12	3°29'N 72°53'E
Ribudhoo (I)	Dhaalu	15	2°56'N 72°54'E
Rihiveli (R)	Kaafu	10	3°49'N 73°24'E
Rihiveli (Wk)	Kaafu	10	3°49'N 73°24'E
Riyaala (Wk)	Gaafu Alifu	19	0°46'N 73°08'E
Rodhuvahrenaa (U)	Gaafu Dhaalu	20	0°18'N 73°28'E
Royal Family (Wk)	Haa Dhaalu	3	6°46'N 72°55'E
Royal Island (R)	Baa	7	5°10'N 73°03'E
Ruffushi (U)	Haa Dhaalu	3	6°46'N 72°56'E
Ruhhurihuraa (U)	Vaavu	13	3°22'N 73°30'E
Ruththibirah (U)	Thaa	17	2°10'N 73°03'E
Savaaheli (U)	Seenu	22	0°41'S 73°07'E
Seedhihuraa (U)	Meemu	16	2°52'N 73°34'E
Seedhihuraa Veligandu (U)	Meemu	16	2°52'N 73°34'E
Selhlhifushi (U)	Lhaviyani	8	5°26'N 73°38'E
Shangri-La (R)	Seenu	22	0°41'N 73°12'E
Skipjack 11 (Wk)	Lhaviyani	8	5°29'N 73°24'E
Soneva Fushi (R)	Baa	7	5°07'N 73°04'E
Soneva Gili (R)	Kaafu	9	4°18'N 73°33'E
SS Seagull (Wk)	Kaafu	9	4°46'N 73°30'E
Suaroge (U)	Laamu	18	1°55'N 73°15'E
Summer Island (R)	Kaafu	9	4°32'N 73°22'E
Sun Island (R)	Alifu Dhaalu	12	3°29'N 72°48'E
Swiss (Wk)	Kaafu	9	4°38'N 73°38'E
Taj Coral (R)	Kaafu	9	4°29'N 73°24'E
Taj Exotica (R)	Kaafu	10	4°06'N 73°32'E
Thaavathaa (U)	Raa	6	5°29'N 72°59'E
Thanburudhoo (U)	Kaafu	9	4°19'N 73°35'E
Thanburudhoo Thila (P)	Kaafu	9	4°19'N 73°35'E
Thaburudhoo (U)	Noonu	5	5°43'N 73°14'E
Thaburudhuffushi (U)	Noonu	5	5°43'N 73°14'E
Thackaru (U)	Gaafu Alifu	19	0°37'N 73°12'E
Thakandhoo (I)	Haa Alifu	1	6°51'N 72°59'E

(PR) - Proposed Resort   (R) - Resort   (U) - Uninhabited Island   (I) - Inhabited Island   (WK) - Wreck   (P) - Protected Marine Area

ISLAND NAME	ATOLL	MAP #	REFERENCE
Theefaridhoo (U)	Haa Dhaalu	3	6°44'N 73°02'E
Thelehuttaa (I)	Gaafu Dhaalu	20	0°18'N 73°03'E
Theluveligaa (U)	Alifu Dhaalu	12	3°40'N 72°54'E
Theyofulhihuraa (U)	Alifu Dhaalu	12	3°46'N 72°58'E
Thila Fushi (U)	Kaafu	9	4°11'N 73°26'E
Thilabolhufushi (U)	Dhaalu	15	2°45'N 73°02'E
Thiladhoo (U)	Baa	7	5°16'N 73°09'E
Thilamaafushi (U)	Lhaviyani	8	5°16'N 73°35'E
Thimarafushi (I)	Thaa	17	2°12'N 73°09'E
Thinadhoo (I)	Gaafu Dhaalu	20	0°32'N 73°00'E
Thinadhoo (I)	Vaavu	13	3°29'N 73°32'E
Thinadhoomaahuttaa (U)	Gaafu Dhaalu	20	0°33'N 73°00'E
Thinehuttaa (U)	Gaafu Dhaalu	20	0°22'N 73°02'E
Thinhuraa (U)	Dhaalu	15	2°47'N 73°02'E
Thinkolhufushi (U)	Thaa	17	2°21'N 73°21'E
Thinrukurehaa (U)	Gaafu Alifu	19	0°23'N 73°34'E
Thoddoo (I)	Alifu Alifu	11	4°27'N 72°58'E
Tholhendhoo (I)	Noonu	5	5°55'N 73°27'E
Tholhufushi (U)	Alifu Dhaalu	12	3°29'N 72°47'E
Thoshigadukolhu (U)	Noonu	5	5°44'N 73°25'E
Thulhaadhoo (I)	Baa	7	5°02'N 72°51'E
Thulhaagiri (R)	Kaafu	9	4°18'N 73°29'E
Thulusdhoo (I)	Kaafu	9	4°23'N 73°39'E
Thunburi (U)	Laamu	18	2°04'N 73°33'E
Thundudhoshu Finolhu (U)	Laamu	18	2°01'N 73°22'E
Thundufushi (R)	Alifu Dhaalu	12	3°47'N 72°44'E
Thunduhuraa (U)	Vaavu	13	3°21'N 73°31'E
Thuraakunu (I)	Haa Alifu	1	7°06'N 72°54'E
Thuvaru (U)	Meemu	16	2°54'N 73°23'E
Twin Island (R)	Alifu Dhaalu	12	3°37'N 72°54'E
Udhdhoo (U)	Dhaalu	15	2°58'N 72°59'E
Ufulandhoo (U)	Raa	6	5°28'N 72°55'E
Ufulingili (U)	Baa	7	5°01'N 72°58'E
Ufuriyaa (U)	Thaa	17	2°22'N 73°22'E
Ugulifinolhu (U)	Haa Alifu	1	6°58'N 72°54'E
Uhehuttaa (U)	Gaafu Dhaalu	20	0°13'N 73°11'E
Uherehaa (U)	Gaafu Alifu	19	0°24'N 73°34'E
Ukulhas (I)	Alifu Alifu	11	4°13'N 72°52'E
Ukurihuttaa (U)	Gaafu Dhaalu	20	0°14'N 73°07'E
Ulegalaa (U)	Gaafu Dhaalu	20	0°24'N 73°22'E
Uligamu (I)	Haa Alifu	1	7°05'N 72°56'E
Umaana (Wk)	Gaafu Alifu	19	0°50'N 73°25'E
Umarefinolhu (U)	Haa Alifu	1	7°01'N 72°51'E
Undoodhoo (U)	Baa	7	5°17'N 73°03'E
Ungoofaaru (I)	Raa	6	5°40'N 73°02'E
Ungulu (U)	Raa	6	5°42'N 73°02'E
Usfushi (U)	Thaa	17	2°15'N 73°13'E
Utheemu (I)	Haa Alifu	1	6°50'N 73°06'E
Uthuruboduveli (U)	Meemu	16	3°02'N 73°37'E
Uthurumaafaru (U)	Raa	6	5°40'N 72°51'E
Uthuruvinagandu (U)	Laamu	18	1°49'N 73°17'E
Uvadhevifushi (U)	Laamu	18	1°59'N 73°32'E
Vaadhoo (I)	Gaafu Dhaalu	20	0°14'N 73°16'E
Vaadhoo (I)	Raa	6	5°52'N 72°59'E
Vadoo (R)	Kaafu	10	4°08'N 73°28'E
Vaagali (U)	Kaafu	10	3°57'N 73°22'E
Vaanee (I)	Dhaalu	15	2°43'N 73°00'E
Vabbinfaru (U)	Kaafu	9	4°18'N 73°26'E
Vabboahuraa (R)	Kaafu	9	4°19'N 73°36'E
Vadinolhu (U)	Laamu	18	2°01'N 73°22'E
Vaffushi (U)	Raa	6	5°38'N 72°51'E
Vaffushihuraa (U)	Raa	6	5°38'N 72°52'E
Vagaaru (U)	Haa Alifu	1	7°06'N 72°53'E
Vagaru (PR)	Shaviyani	4	6°05'N 73°12'E
Vaikaradhoo (I)	Haa Dhaalu	3	6°33'N 72°57'E
Vaikaramuraidhoo (U)	Haa Dhaalu	3	6°33'N 72°54'E

ISLAND NAME	ATOLL	MAP #	REFERENCE
Vaireyaadhuvaa (U)	Gaafu Dhaalu	20	0°17'N 73°20'E
Vakarufalhi (R)	Alifu Dhaalu	12	3°34'N 72°54'E
Vakkaru (U)	Baa	7	5°08'N 72°59'E
Valla (U)	Dhaalu	15	2°43'N 72°53'E
Valla-Ihohi (U)	Dhaalu	15	2°44'N 72°53'E
Valtur Kihaad (R)	Baa	7	5°12'N 73°08'E
Vammaafushi (U)	Kaafu	10	3°57'N 73°30'E
Vanbadhi (U)	Thaa	17	2°11'N 72°59'E
Vandhoo (U)	Thaa	17	2°18'N 72°57'E
Vandhoo (U)	Raa	6	5°32'N 73°03'E
Varihuraa (U)	Lhaviyani	8	5°18'N 73°29'E
Vashafaru (I)	Haa Alifu	1	6°54'N 73°09'E
Vashahera (U)	Seenu	22	0°41'S 73°08'E
Vashavarrehaa (PR)	Gaafu Dhaalu	20	0°15'N 73°18'E
Vashugiri (R)	Vaavu	13	3°38'N 73°22'E
Vattaru (U)	Noonu	5	5°40'N 73°23'E
Vattaru (U)	Vaavu	13	3°14'N 73°26'E
Vattaru Kandu (P)	Vaavu	13	3°14'N 73°26'E
Vavathi (U)	Noonu	5	5°48'N 73°13'E
Vavvaru (U)	Lhaviyani	8	5°25'N 73°22'E
Velassaru (R)	Kaafu	10	4°07'N 73°26'E
Velavaru (R)	Dhaalu	15	2°59'N 73°01'E
Velidhoo (I)	Noonu	5	5°40'N 73°17'E
Velidhu (R)	Alifu Alifu	11	4°12'N 72°49'E
Velifinolhu (U)	Haa Alifu	1	6°59'N 72°52'E
Veligadu (U)	Lhaviyani	8	5°31'N 73°26'E
Veligadufinolhu (U)	Laamu	18	1°50'N 73°24'E
Veligandu (R)	Alifu Alifu	11	4°18'N 73°02'E
Veligandu (U)	Haa Dhaalu	3	6°45'N 72°56'E
Veligandu Huraa (R)	Kaafu	10	3°58'N 73°31'E
Veraaviligillaa (U)	Gaafu Dhaalu	20	0°19'N 73°27'E
Veriheiybe (U)	Meemu	16	3°02'N 73°37'E
Veymandhoo (I)	Thaa	17	2°11'N 73°06'E
Veyofushi (U)	Baa	7	5°14'N 73°09'E
Veyvah (I)	Meemu	16	2°57'N 73°36'E
Veyvah (U)	Lhaviyani	8	5°26'N 73°22'E
Veyvah (U)	Raa	6	5°46'N 72°54'E
Vicissitude (Wk)	Haa Alifu	1	7°07'N 72°49'E
Vihafarufinolhu (U)	Lhaviyani	8	5°27'N 73°35'E
Vihafarufinolhu (U)	Noonu	5	5°41'N 73°17'E
Vihamaafaru (I)	Alifu Alifu	11	4°07'N 72°44'E
Vihamanaafushi (U)	Kaafu	9	4°13'N 73°31'E
Vilamendhoo (R)	Alifu Dhaalu	12	3°38'N 72°58'E
Viligalaa (U)	Gaafu Alifu	19	0°32'N 73°19'E
Villigili (I)	Gaafu Alifu	19	0°45'N 73°26'E
Villingili (I)	Kaafu	9	4°11'N 73°29'E
Villingili (PR)	Seenu	22	0°41'S 73°12'E
Viligili (U)	Raa	6	5°23'N 72°57'E
Viligilimathidhahuraa (U)	Kaafu	9	4°23'N 73°40'E
Viligilivaru (U)	Alifu Dhaalu	12	3°37'N 72°58'E
Viligilivaru (U)	Kaafu	10	3°55'N 73°27'E
Viligilivarufinolhu (U)	Faafu	14	3°17'N 73°00'E
Villivaru (R)	Kaafu	10	3°55'N 73°27'E
Vilu Reef (R)	Dhaalu	15	3°00'N 73°00'E
Vilufushi (I)	Thaa	17	2°30'N 73°19'E
Vinaneiyfaruhuraa (U)	Baa	7	5°21'N 73°05'E
Voavah (U)	Baa	7	5°19'N 73°04'E
Vodamulaa (U)	Gaafu Alifu	19	0°36'N 73°29'E
Vommuli (U)	Dhaalu	15	2°55'N 72°52'E
W. Retreat & Spa (R)	Alifu Alifu	11	4°00'N 72°49'E
Wakkaru (U)	Raa	6	5°29'N 72°57'E
White Sands (R)	Alifu Dhaalu	12	3°30'N 72°54'E
Wooden Wreck (Wk)	Kaafu	9	4°37'N 73°35'E
Ziyaaraiyfushi (U)	Kaafu	9	4°32'N 73°22'E
Ziyaaraiyfushi (U)	Laamu	18	1°59'N 73°18'E

(PR) - Proposed Resort   (R) - Resort   (U) - Uninhabited Island   (I) - Inhabited Island   (WK) - Wreck   (P) - Protected Marine Area

Dhivehi (Maldivian) Words and Phrases

NUMERALS

One .... *Eheh*
Two .... *Dheiy*
Three .... *Thineh*
Four .... *Hathareh*
Five .... *Faheh*
Six .... *Haeh*
Seven .... *Hatheh*
Eight .... *Asheh*
Nine .... *Nuvaeh*
Ten .... *Dhihaeh*

WEEKDAYS

Monday .... *Hoama*
Tuesday .... *Angaara*
Wednesday ..... *Budha*
Thursday .... *Buraasfathi*
Friday .... *Hukuru*
Saturday .... *Honihiru*
Sunday .... *Aadheet'tha*

TIME

Day .... *Dhuvas*
Noon .... *Mendhuruh*
Evening .... *Haveeru*
Midnight .... *Mendhamu*
Now .... *Mihaaru*
Yesterday .... *Iyye*
Tomorrow .... *Maadhan*
Morning .... *Hendhunu*
Afternoon ...... *Mendhuru fas*
Night .... *Reygandu*
Dawn .... *Fathis*
Later .... *Fahun*
Today .... *Miadhu*

USEFUL WORDS

Above .... *Matheega*
Across .... *Hurahah*
Again .... *Adhi*
Anchor .... *Nagili*
Beach .... *Athirimathi*
Big .... *Bodu*
Bird .... *Dhooni*
Blood .... *Ley*

Boat .... *Dhoani*
Cold .... *Fini*
Compass .... *Samugaa*
Coral .... *Gaa/Muraka*
Current .... *Oi*
Dive .... *Feenun*
Dolphin .... *Koamas*
Drink, to .... *Boan*
Eat .... *Kaan*
Empty .... *Hus*
Fish .... *Mas*
Fisherman ...... *Masveriya*
Happy .... *Ufaa*
High tide .... *Bodu dhiya*
Horizon .... *Udhares*
Hot .... *Hoonu*
Island .... *Rah/Fushi*
Lagoon .... *Faruthere*
Lobster .... *Ihi*
Long .... *Dhigu*
Low Tide .... *Hiki dhiya*
Mast .... *Kunbu*
Medicine .... *Beys*
Money .... *Faisaa*
Moon .... *Handhu*
Narrow .... *Hani*

Oar .... *Fali*
Ocean .... *Maakandu*
Rain .... *Vissaara*
Rainbow .... *Vissaara dhuni*
Reef .... *Faru*
Rescue .... *Salaamaiykurun*
Rising tide ..... *Foodhey dhiya*
Rope .... *Roanu*
Rudder .... *Hungaanu*
Sandbank .... *Finolhu*
Shell .... *Boli*
Shore .... *Gondu dhoh*
Sky .... *Udu*
Spring tide .... *Foamathi*
Stern .... *Kolhufas*
Storm .... *Koligandu*
Sun .... *Iru*
Swell .... *Baani*
Temperature .... *Fini hoonu min*
Tide .... *Dhiya*
Water .... *Fen*
Waves .... *Raalhu*
Weather .... *Moosun*
Wet .... *Theiy*
Wind .... *Vai*

USEFUL LOCAL TERMS

Atoll .... A group of islands surrounded by a common reef formation
Cona .... Clear area among corals
Falhu .... Lagoon encircled by a reef sometimes with one or more islands inside
Faru .... Large reef partially exposed at low tide
Finolhu .... Island with few or no coconut trees
Fushi .... Big island usually on the outside reef of the atolls
Futtaru .... Reef where waves break
Giri .... Small patch of coral a couple of metres below the surface
Halu .... Clearing in lagoon
Kandu .... Sea inside atoll
Kandu Olhi ... Channel
Maa Kandu ... Sea outside atoll
Thila .... Coral reef a few metres below the surface
Vilu .... Deep area inside lagoon

USEFUL PHRASES

When are you going? .... *Kaley dhanee kon irakun*
Where is it? .... *E Kobaa*
Where are you going? .... *Kaley dhanee kon thaakah*
Be quick .... *Avas kuraathi*
Go ahead .... *Kuriah dhey*
Go slow .... *Madun dhey*
How much? .... *Kihaa vareh*
How are you? .... *Haalu kihineh*
Thank you .... *Shukuriyyaa*
Watch out .... *Balaathi*
What is it? .... *Eee kon echcheh*
What is the matter? .... *Kihineh vee*
What time are we going? .... *Aharemen dhanee kon irakun*
How long does it take? .... *Kihaa ireh nagaanee*
What is that island? .... *E othee kon rasheh*
What is the name of this reef? ... *Mi farah kiyanee kon nameh*
Which way is the current? ...... *Oi othee kon thaakah*
Excuse me I'm sorry .... *Maafu kurey*
Be careful .... *Faruvaa bahattaathi*
I see .... *Ehen dhoa*
Yes .... *Aanh/ladda/aadhe*
No .... *Noon*
What time is it? .... *Gadin kihaa ireh*